1982

A GALLERY OF SINISTER PERSPECTIVES

Albert Borowitz

A GALLERY OF SINISTER PERSPECTIVES

Ten Crimes and a Scandal

The Kent State University Press

Portions of this work, in somewhat different form, appeared originally in *Opera News, California Law Review, The Armchair Detective, The American Bar Association Journal, The Music Review,* and *The Victorian Newsletter.* "The Trial of Jane's Aunt" first appeared in *Chilling and Killing,* an anthology edited by Joan Kahn (New York: Houghton Mifflin, 1978).

Frontispiece: Detail from *Parte del Foro di Nerva* by Giovanni Battista Piranesi.

Design by Harold M. Stevens

Library of Congress Cataloging in Publication Data

Borowitz, Albert, 1930–
   A gallery of sinister perspectives.

   Bibliography: p.
   Contents: The ring and the book and the murder —
Portraits of Beatrice — Innocence and arsenic —
[etc.]
   1. Crime and criminals in literature—Addresses,
essays, lectures.   2. Crime and criminals—Addresses,
essays, lectures.   I. Title.
PN56.C7B59   809'.93355   81-19352
ISBN 0-87338-264-1   AACR2

To Helen . . .

CONTENTS

Preface

> Continue to beckon me along the gallery that I can't tread alone, and where, by your leave, I link my arm confraternally in yours: the gallery of sinister perspective just stretches in this manner straight away.
>
> *Henry James, letter to the*
> *crime historian William Roughead*

In this collection, I pursue the two special interests that were marked out in my first book, *Innocence and Arsenic: Studies in Crime and Literature* (Harper & Row, 1977): criminal cases and traditions in which writers, musicians, or intellectuals have been involved either as actual participants or observers or as the subjects of accusations or legends; and crimes that have inspired significant works of literature or music. My recent study of the Manning case of 1849, *The Woman Who Murdered Black Satin: The Bermondsey Horror* (Columbus: Ohio State University Press, 1981), shows both strands of this subject matter closely interwoven. Dickens as observer attended the Mannings' trial and execution, the latter provoking his masterly letters to the *London Times* advocating an end to public hanging. A few years later, Dickens as novelist assimilated and reworked the personality and gestures of Mrs. Manning as the raw material for his portrayal of the murderess Mlle. Hortense in *Bleak House*.

Four essays in the present book illustrate direct confrontations between creative artists or intellectuals and crime. In "Innocence and Arsenic: The Literary and Criminal Careers of C. J. L. Almquist," a distinguished nineteenth-century Swedish writer appears in the unusual role of a convicted would-be murderer. (This essay was originally intended to be included in my 1977 collection, which bears its name.) The artist-criminal is for me one of the most beguiling figures in crime history, since he raises a number of unyielding issues. Of these, the foremost is the problem posed by Pushkin at the end of his play *Mozart and Salieri*: to what extent are genius and criminality compatible? In the career of Almquist this question emerges in a more disturbing variant: can the very inner forces that fuel literary imagination also cause a weakened sense of reality to misgovern the external behavior of the writer?

Closely related to the few documented cases of artist-criminals are the instances in which tradition has, generally without any justification, branded an artist as a murderer. In this genre the Mozart-Salieri poisoning myth has recently won revived fame. My essay on that subject (included in my first book) is, I believe, the most detailed study in English; Peter Shaffer's play *Amadeus* has now made the old slander against Salieri a household word. However, dark legends involving homicidal musicians antedate Mozart's time. In the present work, "Lully and the Death of Cambert" recounts another chapter in murder folklore from the music worlds of seventeenth-century Paris and London. As in the case of the accusations against Salieri, this earlier legend stemmed from the intense competitiveness of musicians and, more particularly, from the understandable rivalry of opera composers vying for limited performance opportunities.

It is only natural that a student of the crimes of brilliant people will propound another question: are they as ingenious in the perpetration of murder as in their nobler pursuits? The answer is disappointing, for the artist or intellectual is often observed to be a bungling criminal. In *A Gallery of Sinister Perspectives* this homely truth is demonstrated by Almquist's ludicrous poisoning attempts and by the failure of the talented Harvard chemist and professor John W. Webster to obliterate the remains of his victim ("The Janitor's Story: An Ethical Dilemma in the Harvard Murder Case"). Perhaps even the genius should stick to his last and leave crime to the professionals.

Fortunately, men and women of genius who have participated in criminal cases usually play a more constructive role; they have often appeared as advocates, either out of professional obligation or for considerations of personal loyalty or ideological conviction. The noble tradition of the writer in combat for justice has embraced the crusades of Emile Zola and Arthur Conan Doyle, and in our own times the campaign of Arthur Miller to vindicate Peter Reilly. In "The Case of A Yün," two of the foremost thinkers of Sung China, historian Ssu-ma

Kuang and social reformer Wang An-shih match their powers of literary expression and legal persuasion in a struggle to win the emperor to their respective views of justice in the case of a country girl charged with an assault on her unwelcome fiancé. The brilliant seventeenth-century letter writer Mme. de Sévigné was a devoted partisan of the cause of her close friend, Nicolas Fouquet, the fallen finance minister of Louis XIV charged with treason and embezzlement of State funds. Her letters describing Fouquet's trial are replete with political and legal insight and also candidly reveal an effort to bring her considerable personal influence and charm to bear on the outcome of the court proceedings. By contrast with Mme. de Sévigné's active sideline monitoring of Fouquet's trial, Jane Austen's reaction to her Aunt Jane Leigh Perrot's prosecution for shoplifting is a matter for speculation, since at her aunt's insistence she was not permitted to attend the court sessions. However, it is the conclusion of "The Trial of Jane's Aunt" that Mrs. Leigh Perrot's ordeal has left its traces in the pages of her famous niece's novels.

The impact of factual crime on works of literature and music, the second principal subject of my writing, is, of course, a much broader category than the history of direct participation by authors and artists in criminal cases. As early as 1592, we find in *Arden of Feversham* an English drama closely patterned on the lurid facts of a family murder, and its progeny have been countless. An attempt to survey the immense debt of theatre and fiction to crime history (the "gallery of sinister perspective," as Henry James called it in an admiring letter to his friend, the Scottish crime writer William Roughead) would be beyond the reach of bibliography, not to mention literary analysis. However, no serious study of landmarks of crime literature can fail to pay respect to Robert Browning's *The Ring and the Book*, perhaps the most persuasive assertion of the power of the creative imagination to free the human facts of crime from the limitations of the trial record. In "The Ring and the Book and the Murder" I accept Browning's sermon that lawyers do not have a monopoly over the quest for the truth about crime. A similar lesson is, in fact, urged in " 'Under Sentence of Death': Some Literary Views on Capital Punishment," in which it is suggested that the literature of the last three centuries may have as much to tell us about the death penalty as our own judges and econometrics experts.

An earlier analogue to the seventeenth-century Italian murder case that inspired *The Ring and the Book* is the immortal conspiracy of Beatrice Cenci and her brothers against their father, Francesco. My chapter "Portraits of Beatrice" traces the literary and musical transformations of the Cenci tragedy from Shelley's poetic drama to Alberto Ginastera's opera that was performed at the New York City Opera in 1973. No better example can be cited of the manner in which a classic crime, when studied through the ages by artists of sensibility, can serve as a touchstone of changing social attitudes.

Crime of the late nineteenth century is represented in the collection by an essay in a lighter vein. In "Gilbert and Sullivan on Corporation Law: *Utopia, Limited* and the Panama Canal Frauds" I point out (apparently for the first time) the direct inspiration of the late Savoyard opera by the Panama Canal fraud case that was proceeding in Paris in the year of *Utopia*'s premiere (1893). The excesses of the Canal's promoters confirmed the wildest fantasies of business abuses that Gilbert, a failed barrister, had scattered throughout the pages of his earlier librettos. The ever darkening era of contemporary crime is reflected in my study of the manifold true-crime sources of *Night Must Fall* by Emlyn Williams, who is a relentless and thoughtful student of modern murder cases.

Even in a collection devoted to the literature of crime, it is appropriate that death and punishment should take a brief holiday. I have therefore rounded out the dozen entries in the book with an account of the celebrated quarrel of Dickens and Thackeray, which, with apologies to Dorothy Sayers, I have called "The Unpleasantness at the Garrick Club." Though no blows were struck, the furor at the Garrick Club had all the characteristics of a great mystery story—strong antagonists, a slowly gathering storm, and an explosive denouement. For me, the affair has a special poignancy: it brought into conflict my two favorite English writers.

The Ring and the Book and the Murder

It is said that you can't make a silk purse out of a sow's ear, and yet a great literature has been created about murder and crime. In making this claim I would not be taken to exaggerate the literary merits of Agatha Christie and Erle Stanley Gardner. If we place these popular writers low in the critical scale, it may be because they ask and answer the least interesting questions about crime. The classic question is, of course, "who-dun-it," and the answer, depending on the ingenuity of the author, may range from the butler to the reader himself. Edmund Wilson has given the response of many serious booklovers to the most famous "who-dun-it" posed by Miss Christie by entitling his savage essay on detective fiction "Who Cares Who Killed Roger Ackroyd?"

A second traditional puzzle pattern of the orthodox detective novel has been sometimes referred to as the "how-dun-it," that is, a narrative where the mystery arises mainly from the culprit's use of a unique murder weapon or method. We are all familiar with the gun concealed in the baby grand and primed to go off when the concert pianist plays his chronically wrong E-flat. This kind of plot is often enthralling, but of limited educational value, except to the extent that it underscores the importance of hard practice at the keyboard.

Ingenious variations on these themes have been worked out. Pat McGerr in *Pick Your Victim* (1947) must be credited with the invention of the "whom-was-it-dun-to": a group of marines at an isolated wartime base in the Aleutians read a torn news article about the murder confession of a friend and try to determine which member of their social circle was done in. Another new path was opened in Mary Kelly's *Due To a Death* (1962). In this novel, which might be styled a "what-was-dun," we only learn at the very end what crime has been committed.

However, in speaking of a great literature of crime, I am not referring to the annual bumper crops of the "who-dun-its" and their variants but to a genre that may be called the "why-dun-its," that is, to works where the identity of the criminal and victim may be known at the outset or at least comes as no great surprise, the means of death is commonplace, and the primary questions relate to the murderer's motives and the significance of the crime to the community. It is appropriate to borrow from Raymond Chandler's praise of his master, Dashiell Hammett, by saying that this category of crime writing "[gives] murder back to the kind of people that commit it for reasons, not just to provide a corpse; and with the means at hand, not with hand-wrought duelling pistols . . . and tropical fish."

Crime literature of the "why-dun-it" variety includes both fiction and nonfiction, and other works that fall somewhere in between—the so-called "nonfiction novels" or "new journalism." Much of this literature, regardless of whether the fictional or nonfictional mode predominates, is based on, or to some extent inspired by, the facts of actual crimes and trials. To explain why this is so, one may, of course, have recourse to Byron's observation that "truth is stranger than fiction." This adage is pertinent to the field of crime in the sense that certain of the classic cases that crime writers have described involve murders more bizarre in their conception and execution than any that owe their origins to the pens of Ellery Queen or John Dickson Carr. However, the most significant respect in which crime history may be stranger than fiction is that the motivations of the real-life murderer are usually more complex and ambiguous than his counterparts in the pages of who-dun-its. Crime annals teach us that murder, the gravest human offense, is often committed for rewards or impelled by motives that appear to be less substantial or less comprehensible than those that have incited men to lesser crimes. Though a fully satisfying explanation of a criminal's actions may ultimately elude us, rich resources for speculation about human conduct are often provided by the extraordinarily detailed testimony and documentation to be found in the records of investigations and trials.

One of the most eloquent appraisals of the unique treasures that may be mined from the study of crime history was written by Friedrich Schiller in his introduction to a popular German edition of *causes célèbres* published in 1792:

> We catch sight here of people in the most complicated situations, which keep us in total suspense and whose *dénouements* provide pleasant employment

for the reader's ability to predict the outcome. The secret play of passion unfolds before our eyes, and many a ray of truth is cast over the hidden paths of intrigue. The springs of conduct, which in everyday life are concealed from the eye of the observer, stand out more clearly in motives where life, freedom and property are at stake, and therefore the criminal judge is in a position to have deeper insights into the human heart.

As this passage reveals, crime annals attracted Schiller because, unlike much of the fiction of his day, they offered a combination of powerful narrative suspense and unusually vivid psychological insights. Although he did not deceive himself that any crime is completely explicable, he was a strong believer in the capability of judicial inquiry to arrive at a rational elucidation of human behavior, and accordingly regarded knowledgeable summaries of criminal trials as likely to come closer to an accurate rendering of cause and effect than the most painstaking study of broader historical events.

From the nineteenth century onward the scope of crime literature has immensely expanded as our understanding of irrational behavior has deepened and as we have had to confront an increasing incidence of murders committed out of what Coleridge (in reference to Iago's crimes) called "motiveless malignity." In his 1854 essay "Three Memorable Murders," Thomas De Quincey wrote the first important study in English of an insane urban mass killer, John Williams, the Ratcliffe Highway Murderer. His imaginative reconstruction of the massacre of two London households brought his narrative to a pitch of suspense that would have delighted Schiller; at the same time he attempted to mirror the emotions of the terrorized city and to plumb Williams's dark compulsion to annihilate. The crime literature that has followed De Quincey has approached its subject matter from all the vantage points from which human conduct may be appropriately viewed. Some writers have continued to explore the psychological or philosophical implications of murder. Others are primarily interested in the historical or political significance of criminal cases. Devotees of social history have looked to the light that microscopic examination of a crime and its setting may shed so clearly on the environment, manners, morals and sensibility of a particular society or era. Many lawyers and other writers with knowledge of law have placed their main emphasis on the functions and limitations of the legal process as a means of assessing and judging human conduct. It is a special value of Robert Browning's *The Ring and the Book* (1868–69), and a basis of its honored place in imaginative crime literature, that Browning successfully brings many of these approaches to bear on the antique criminal case that his poem recreates.

In book 1 of *The Ring and the Book* Browning rejects the idea that legal procedure and legal thinking have a monopoly over the search for the truth about human actions. Using a rather painful dental pun, he ironically refers to the law as "the patent truth-extracting process" (book 1, line 1114; subsequent references are to book and line numbers). Against the claims that the legal profession makes to expertise in fact-finding, Browning asserts the competitive claims of the creative imagination, of fictional reconstruction, and of poetry.

The Ring and the Book is a long narrative poem that follows, for the most part with scrupulous accuracy, the events of a triple murder committed by Count Guido Franceschini and four henchmen in Rome in 1698. Because I will later refer to some of the events of the crime in greater detail, I had better begin, as lawyers are accustomed to do, with a brief statement of the case.

The principal defendant, Guido, was a poor nobleman from Arezzo in Tuscany. He had gone to Rome to seek his fortune and served as secretary to a cardinal. But he had entered his forties without having obtained either distinction or financial success. Then he married Pompilia Comparini, the thirteen-year-old daughter of a well-to-do Roman middle-class couple. Guido's motives for entering this marriage may be a subject for controversy, but there is no doubt that it turned out to be another unsuccessful venture. He brought his child-bride and her parents home to his family mansion. Soon dissension developed between Guido and Pompilia's parents, and they returned to Rome leaving their daughter behind. Whatever the rights and wrongs of this family dispute may have been, Pompilia's parents, once back at home, took a step that was certainly not designed to charm their son-in-law. They publicly announced that Pompilia was not their daughter after all, but the daughter of a Roman prostitute. On the basis of this claim they instituted legal proceedings against Count Guido to recover their dowry (2.549–602).

Meanwhile, Pompilia was very unhappy with her husband. Under circumstances that were later to be the subject of considerable legal dispute, she arranged to flee to Rome in the company of Guiseppe Caponsacchi, a young nobleman of Arezzo who held the ecclesiastical office of canon. Count Guido intercepted the two fugitives en route. A prosecution was then instituted in Rome against Pompilia and Caponsacchi for elopement and adultery. It is not clear what the court's conclusion was as to the more interesting of the two charges, but the two defendants were punished very lightly, Caponsacchi being confined to a small town near Rome for three years and Pompilia being placed, perhaps without any formal judgment, in an institution for penitent women (3.1376–1418).

About one month later, Pompilia was released to the custody of her parents and shortly thereafter, on December 18, 1697, gave birth to a son. The news of the birth appears to have enraged Count Guido further. On the evening of January 2, 1698, Guido and four armed accomplices went to the house of Pompilia's parents and murdered them together with the young mother. The five assassins were tried, convicted, and executed for their crime in February 1698.

In summarizing the main events that form the basis of Browning's poem, I have tried to state the facts that are not disputed. Browning is a determined adversary, however, and does not readily permit any facts to be withdrawn from the arena of contention. Indeed, one of the most fascinating aspects of *The Ring and the Book* is the poet's insistence that the truth about human behavior does not consist of a single accurate statement from which all inconsistencies are sifted out and excluded. In Browning's view, to render a mature judgment on a human dispute one must first allow the actors in the drama to place their own widely varying interpretations on the actions and motives of themselves and their enemies, and one must also listen to the highly partisan arguments of the professional and lay adherents to the parties in the dispute. In order, in the words of G. K. Chesterton, to "depict the various strange ways in which a fact gets itself presented to the world," Browning tells the story of Guido's crime from the points of view of nine narrators: the pro-Guido man in the street ("Half-Rome"); the anti-Guido man in the street (the "Other Half-Rome"); the sophisticated newsreader ("Tertium Quid") who knows the issues but leaves the decisions to the professionals; Count Guido himself; Caponsacchi; Pompilia; counsel for the defense; counsel for the prosecution; and the Pope, who considered and rejected Guido's appeal.

As examples of the ferocious divergence of Browning's narrators on the facts of the case, two crucial issues may be cited: (1) Did Pompilia write certain love letters to her rescuer, Caponsacchi, that were placed in evidence, or, indeed, could she write at all? (2) What was the significance of the ruse that Guido used to gain entrance to the murder house? As principal antagonists on these issues I will choose the pro-Guido and anti-Guido man in the street. I cite these narrators because they are purely of Browning's creation and because they may be taken to represent a layman's reaction to legal issues and possibly (although we would hope for less partisanship) the reaction of a juror to the presentation of a case.

The pro-Guido man in the street is a married man who thinks women should be kept in their place. He makes fun of Pompilia's claim of illiteracy and cannot reconcile it with what he conceives to be another fact—that she admitted receipt of letters from Caponsacchi. Nor does he think Pompilia's claim is consistent with Caponsacchi's admission that he received letters that he believed to be from Pompilia (2.1126–60). Yet none of these "facts" seems to damage Pompilia's claim in the slightest. The letters from Caponsacchi, if received, may have been read to her; the alleged letters from her may have been forged by Guido, as was indeed charged (2.1143–47).

The anti-Guido man in the street is a bachelor who apparently has a soft spot in his heart for the young Pompilia. To him it is clear that the alleged love letters were forged by Guido:

> Love-letters from his wife who cannot write
> Love-letters in reply o' the priest—thank God—
> Who can write and confront his character
> With this, and prove the false thing forged throughout . . .
>
> (3.1310–13)

It is interesting to compare these two extreme fictional points of view on the issue of Pompilia's literacy and the composition of the letters with the position taken by the prosecution at the actual trial. In noting Browning's departure from the trial record, we must appreciate, of course, that the goal of the prosecution differed from that of the fictitious anti-Guido man in the street. The prosecution was not necessarily interested in affirmatively proving Pompilia's innocence of adultery but only in showing the unavailability to Guido of a defense of justifiable homicide. Moreover, counsel for the prosecution showed the valid professional concern, quite absent from Browning's man in the street, of not attempting to prove more than they thought the court could be persuaded to believe. Thus, they did not argue strongly that Pompilia was illiterate but contented themselves with the technical position that authorship of the alleged love letters had not been proved by the defense. Apparently believing that the court might attribute the letters to Pompilia, however, the prosecution's counsel pushed their argument further: (1) the letters, even if written by Pompilia, did not provide sufficient evidence that an adulterous affair was being carried on; and (2) even if the terms of the letters were more amorous than would ordinarily be expected in the correspondence of a married woman with the local canon, Pompilia was merely faking romantic interest in order to lure Caponsacchi into rescuing her from her cruel husband. Quite likely, these arguments would have irritated both the pro- and anti-Guido factions, as Browning has depicted them.

Another example of a conflict between the pro-Guido partisan and his anti-Guido counterpart is provided by their interpretations of the fact that Guido and his accomplices gained admittance into the murder house by knocking on the door and announcing the name of Caponsacchi. In their comments on this issue we see these two partisans differing little on the basic fact of what Guido did. Instead, each narrator, on the basis of his own prejudices about the rights and wrongs of the case, constructs elaborate and over-strained inferences as to the significance of Guido's ruse in determining his motives and the guilt or innocence of Pompilia.

The pro-Guido layman says that after knocking on the door, Guido paused and decided to give Pompilia one last chance to prove herself innocent of adultery. Guido believed, he says, that if Pompilia had not had illicit relations with Caponsacchi she would refuse to open the door on his name being called. With this intention of giving Pompilia an opportunity to save her life by proving her good morals, Guido, according to the version of his partisans, shouted "Giuseppe Caponsacchi," and the door flew open (2.1405–32).

The anti-Guido partisan believes that the message at the door was itself less compromising; it did not announce a personal visit by Caponsacchi but " 'A friend of Caponsacchi's bringing friends/A letter' " (3.1598–99). Moreover, the inferences as to Pompilia's guilt are flatly rejected. Her partisan reasons that (1) being a new mother, if Caponsacchi's name had inspired her with any guilt or shame, she would not have opened the door (3.1601–6); and (2) if, as had been rumored, Caponsacchi had been visiting her secretly, he would have entered the home stealthily and by password, so that Pompilia would have been suspicious at the open announcement of his name (3.1607–12). Moreover, in the mind of Pompilia's partisan, Guido's use of Caponsacchi's name affirmatively proved that Guido knew Caponsacchi was not visiting Pompilia or else he would have feared that Caponsacchi might be inside at the very moment and the ruse accordingly frustrated (3.1613–14). Thus the inferences are reversed, Pompilia exonerated of adultery and Guido's role of a husband retrieving his honor rejected.

The reasonings of the two partisans about the knock on the door may strike us first as very ingenious, but even brief reflection will show that they make no logical sense at all and are purely arbitrary conclusions based on the prejudices of the speakers. Thus the pro-Guido spokesman assumes that if Pompilia opened the door to Caponsacchi she must have had an illicit affair with him. Yet it is obvious that even if she were innocent of adultery she would owe a debt of gratitude to Caponsacchi as her rescuer and would not shut the door in his face. On the other hand, the anti-Guido spokesman assumes that if Caponsacchi had been paying visits to Pompilia he would have entered the house by use of a password, and thus the door would not have been opened when Guido used the ruse of announcing Caponsacchi's name. The weakness of this inference is obvious when we recall that Pompilia was living in her parents' home; that her parents were accused by Guido of having encouraged their daughter's elopement; and that, if this accusation was true, Caponsacchi would not have had to use any passwords to find an ample welcome in Pompilia's home.

Bewildering as these two versions of the "knock on the door" incident may strike us, we are to be further perplexed when we are later presented with two inconsistent versions by Guido himself. In his first monologue, Guido seems to support his adherent's version by stating that he pronounced Caponsacchi's name as "the predetermined touch for truth" (5.1629). But in his second monologue, as he awaits his execution, he recalls only that as he knocked on the door he was afraid that some neighbors might be inside visiting Pompilia and the baby and might summon aid, or that one of the three intended victims might escape (11.1582–99).

In giving examples of conflicts in the Browning testimony, I have discussed issues turning on authenticity of documents and evidence of an oral statement at the Comparinis' door, and have not considered the more significant conflicts on issues of motivation, morals, and psychology. After being led through the thicket of these deeper conflicts, one can sympathize to some extent with Browning's statement in the last book of the poem that the lesson of *The Ring and the Book* is that

> . . . our human speech is naught,
> Our human testimony false, our fame
> And human estimation words and wind.
> (12.834–36)

But this summation is a misrepresentation of the poem's achievement. Browning is not saying that there is no truth and no falsehood in the murder case; if he were to do so his claims at the beginning of the poem as to the truth-seeking power of art would have proved a false advertisement. It is true that on many of the factual issues of the case we never receive Browning's findings. It is true also that the poet has emphasized the importance of the witness's point of view and the bad man's ability to say more for himself than one might have imagined possible. But it is wrong to conclude from this that Browning is teaching that there is no reality apart from the witness's viewpoint. In this respect we must contrast him with some of our modern relativists, like the Italian dramatist Pirandello, who answers questions on even the most concrete factual points with the statement, "Right You Are! If You Think You Are!"

Browning, unlike Pirandello, appears to make a judgment on the case and to find Guido guilty. He is not concerned with Guido's legal guilt, however, but with what G. K. Chesterton, in his essay on the poem, has called "spiritual guilt." To Browning, Guido was guilty of renouncing the power to feel or inspire love in favor of an empty pursuit of a career and of wealth; he was guilty in his assumption that his noble birth guaranteed him certain rewards withheld from common men and exempted him from their moral code. The contrast between Browning's judgment and the judgment of the legal process in the historical trial is striking and discomfiting. Guido was apparently convicted at the trial because, even assuming Pompilia had committed adultery, (1) he did not satisfy himself with killing his wife but killed her parents as well, (2) he did not do the deed alone but conspired with four men, and (3) he and his accomplices carried murder weapons shorter than permitted by statute.

The potential existence of broad gaps between legal guilt and the moral, spiritual guilt that Browning considered in this poem has remained an obsessive theme for the writers of our own time. As one of many available examples, we may refer to the criminal in Albert Camus' *The Stranger*, who is convicted legally for murder but spiritually for his inability to feel the emotions that the community feels.

Wholly apart from issues of the guilt of Guido, Browning's version of the trial, particularly in the monologue of the Pope, takes on a social, political, and religious significance that is, quite properly, not within the scope of the pleadings that counsel made in behalf of Guido's prosecution and defense. The Pope sees in Guido's career evidence of an outgrowth of a materialistic age which promises more than it can deliver. He says of the defendant: "So, Guido, born with appetite, lacks food" (12.835). Study of the case also leads the Pope into consideration of the distance that the Church system has moved from the spiritual sources of the Christian religion. This distance is marked by the fact that Guido, whose life and crime showed clearly the complete absence of Christian feeling, appealed to the Pope for reprieve on the ground that he was entitled to exemption from the death penalty as a minor Church official.

It is, of course, quite right that the legal process does not extend its fact-finding to the broad issues of spiritual, institutional, and historical guilt that Browning brings within the range of his speculations. Therefore, the powerful fictive reconstruction of crime history in *The Ring and the Book* does not make its impact upon us by serving as a critique of the procedural shortcomings of legal inquiry. The achievement of the poem, it seems to me, lies in its bringing us to the realization that a criminal case is not the exclusive preserve of its parties, witnesses, lawyers, and judges, that it may have philosophical or social significance that others may be better able to interpret. This lesson is nowhere better illustrated than by the Guido Franceschini trial itself which would have apparently fallen into complete oblivion had not Browning found a soiled report of the case in an Italian bookstall and seen things there that nobody had seen before. In modern times, the Sacco-Vanzetti case provides another example of a criminal prosecution whose significance has radiated far beyond the court records. On the technical level, that trial, of course, presented important issues as to the trustworthiness of eyewitness testimony and the proper limits of examination and argument as to a defendant's political beliefs. But the condemnation and execution of Sacco and Vanzetti have meant a good deal more to our poets, dramatists, and novelists. From such *causes célèbres*, we have gradually learned to accept Browning's persuasive argument that the law does not have a monopoly over the "truth-extracting process"; and that the essential meaning of a criminal case may remain to be elaborated by the writers of succeeding generations.

Portraits of Beatrice: The Cenci Case in Literature and Opera

We are taught that the history of Rome, like the social history of mankind, began with a fratricide. The people of Rome share with us all the inborn feeling that the destruction of one's own flesh and blood is the worst of crimes. It is in part the dread and fascination inspired by family murder that have won a curious immortality for the trial of Beatrice Cenci and her brothers in Rome in 1599 for the murder of their father, Francesco. The trial was a convulsive event and left behind it substantial contemporary commentaries in addition to the official trial records. The interest of the public was understandable. The case was not only a patricide but also an archetypal drama involving generational struggle, a social setting of wealth and nobility, the competing claims of religious authority and individual will, and an aura of violence and of sexual and moral corruption. Beginning with Shelley's great poetry-drama of 1819, a large number of literary and operatic settings have been made of the Cenci tragedy. A recent version is the opera by Alberto Ginastera, *Beatrix Cenci*, which had its American premieres at The Kennedy Center For the Performing Arts in September 1971 and at the New York City Opera in March 1973.

The story of the Cencis turns on the tragic confrontation of the dissolute nobleman, Count Francesco Cenci, and his children. Francesco was bequeathed an ancient Roman lineage and a great fortune by his father, Cristoforo. Francesco's inheritance of the family name was one of those last-minute affairs, since Cristoforo married Francesco's mother only on his deathbed and had legitimated his twelve-year-old son shortly before. Francesco's succession to his father's fortune was even more tenuous, since Cristoforo, as an official of the papal treasury, had made himself rich through embezzlement of Church funds and passed on to his son, together with his wealth, the determination of the Church government to reclaim its rightful portion.

Francesco's youth was stormy and was marked not only by amorous adventure with the women of Rome but also by signs of perversion and a strain of violence that found frequent release in street brawling and attacks on servants and tenants. He was often imprisoned, but fines and money damages won him freedom. Most of his sons grew up in his own image of violence, but he liked them no better for the resemblance. Ironically bearing a surname meaning "rags," Cenci kept his sons in a state of destitution until three of them obtained a papal decree ordering him to provide them with maintenance. Francesco was also caught in a maze of lawsuits with his creditors, who challenged the restrictions he had placed on family properties, and with the Church, to which he twice made reparation for his father's thievery. He was always in litigation with members of his own family, his most sensational controversy being his unsuccessful (but prescient) claim that his son Giacomo was attempting to poison him.

Two of his sons died violently, Rocco being killed in the aftermath of a street fight and Cristoforo being murdered in Trastevere in a love triangle that would have delighted the heart of Mascagni. Tradition has Francesco rejoicing in his sons' deaths, but his joys were numbered. Creditors were closing in on the stingy count and a dowry was required for the marriage of his daughter Antonina. Worst of all, he was convicted in 1594 of sodomy, and saved himself from the stake only by a payment of one-third of his estate to the Roman government.

In 1597, Francesco, with his daughter Beatrice and his second wife, Lucrezia, moved from Rome to the Castle of Petrella, perched high on a crag in the Abbruzzi. The castle was situated in the Kingdom of Naples just beyond the borders of the Papal States; rumor was divided as to whether his purpose in moving was to devise new crimes beyond the reach of vigilant Roman authorities, or, more prosaically, to escape his creditors. In any event, he seemed intent on keeping Beatrice under his control in the castle indefinitely so as to prevent her marriage and the burden of another dowry. What began as residence passed into imprisonment, with Beatrice and her stepmother being confined in a room whose windows were walled up and replaced by air vents. He beat Lucrezia with a riding-spur when she upbraided him for an attempted sexual assault on her young son, and struck Beatrice with a bullwhip after he discovered a letter she had written to her brother Giacomo seeking his help in obtaining her release.

From the violence and degradation to which he subjected his daughter and wife in the castle and from the largely financial grievances of his son Giacomo, a murder conspiracy gradually took form. Beatrice's lawyer, the eminent Prospero Farinaccio, was later to argue unsuccessfully, on the basis of inconclusive and conflicting testimony of two maids, that the principal murder motive was an incestuous attack by Francesco upon Beatrice. The tradition and literature of the case seized on the incest claim as central to the tragedy. But nobody can read of the wretched treatment of the two women at La Petrella without finding Francesco's cruelty to be unnatural even in the absence of incest.

The murder conspiracy may be described as a tragedy of errors. Beatrice appears to have been the main force behind the crime, but the murderer was Olimpio Calvetti, castellan of La Petrella, with whom Beatrice had been having a love affair. Giacomo gave his consent to the murder from Rome but lent little assistance, except a supply of poison that could not be administered to Francesco because of his suspicious nature. Lucrezia wavered, but when the murder hour arrived, it was she who unlocked the door to her husband's bedroom. Assisted by Marzio Catalano, a tinker and sometime guitar teacher, Olimpio killed Francesco with a hammer. The count's body was thrown from the castle after the murderers clumsily enlarged a hole in a balcony in order to make it appear that the floor had given way. Suspicions of murder were immediately aroused, and they were increased by the over-hasty burial of the count and the inept attempts of the conspirators to cover up evidence of the murder. On the orders of the Cenci family and their ally, Monsignore Mario Guerra (whom tradition later incorrectly identified as a suitor of Beatrice), Olimpio was assassinated to eliminate his testimony. However, Olimpio's accomplice Marzio, who had been wandering through neighboring villages giving guitar lessons with Count Cenci's cloak on his back as payment and proof of his crime, was captured and confessed his part in the murder. After initial arrogant denials leading to continued questioning and to torture, Giacomo, Lucrezia and Beatrice ultimately confessed. Giacomo and Lucrezia put the principal blame on Beatrice, and Beatrice blamed her dead lover, Olimpio.

Beatrice, Lucrezia, Giacomo, and a teen-aged brother, Bernardo (who at most may have concurred passively in Giacomo's consent to the murder), were sentenced to death. The brief of their principal defense counsel, Farinaccio, survives. He argued that Beatrice's part in the murder was justified by her father's incestuous assault and by her fear of its repetition. (In a note that he appended to a final edition of his brief prepared years later, Farinaccio conceded that the claim of the act of incest had not been proved.) The lawyer contended that Lucrezia had withdrawn from the conspiracy, and Giacomo, he urged, should not be punished more severely than his sister for coming to her defense. Finally, he argued that Bernardo was entitled to clemency because of his minority and dim-wittedness. Bernardo was only seventeen at the time of the murder, but his mental incapacity was demonstrated by no better evidence than that he had difficulty with his Latin lessons.

All the defendants were condemned to death. It is conjectured that Pope Clement VIII might have been inclined to mercy had not another murder of a noble parent, Costanza Santacroce, entirely without extenuating circumstances, occurred in Rome while he was considering the Cenci case. In any event, the Pope granted a reprieve only to young Bernardo, who was, however, condemned to witness the executions and thereafter to serve in prison galleys.

The executions were cruel. Giacomo was clubbed to death and the two women were beheaded. Beatrice was only twenty-two when she died, but looked younger and is remembered as a beauty. Even at the execution, her unusual hold on the public sympathy and imagination was apparent. Young girls placed garlands on her head while it lay at the foot of the scaffold, and large mourning crowds followed as her body was taken to its resting place in the Church of San Pietro in Montorio. The legend of Beatrice had already begun.

In the seventeenth century fanciful accounts of the case were published that purported to have been written immediately after the executions but may have been written decades later. One such version inspired Shelley to write his drama, *The Cenci*, in 1819. A manuscript purporting to have been copied from the archives of the Cenci Palace was given to the poet during his travels in Italy. In a preface to his play, he recalled that when he arrived in Rome, he "found that the story of the Cenci was a subject not to be mentioned in Italian society without awakening a deep and breathless interest." Shelley was strongly drawn to the figure of Beatrice, "a most gentle and amiable being, a creature formed to adorn and be admired, and thus violently thwarted from her nature by the necessity of circumstance and opinion." At the same time, his anticlerical emotions were aroused by what he saw as evidence of corruption at work in the Pope's judgment. "The old man [the count] had during his life repeatedly bought his pardon from the Pope for capital crimes of the most enormous and unspeakable kind" and the Pope as a consequence "probably felt that whoever killed the Count Cenci deprived his treasury of a certain and copious source of revenue." Shelley even asserted that the Papal government had attempted to suppress the facts relating to its handling of the Cenci case and that the circulation of the manuscript he had received had been "until very lately, a matter of some difficulty."

Shelley intended his play for public performance and even dreamt of

Edmund Kean in the role of Count Francesco. But he recognized that "the story of the Cenci is indeed eminently fearful and monstrous: anything like a dry exhibition of it on the stage would be insupportable." It was necessary, therefore, to "increase the ideal, and diminish the actual horror of the events." As one concession to public taste, Shelley muted the incest theme; Mary Shelley thought the strongest allusion was a curse of Cenci that if Beatrice have a child, it may be

> A hideous likeness of herself, that as
> From a distorting mirror, she may see
> Her image mixed with what she most abhors,
> Smiling upon her from her nursing breast.
> (act 4, scene 1, lines 146–49)

According to Shelley, the highest moral purpose of drama was "the teaching of the human heart, through its sympathies and antipathies, the knowledge of itself." The drama was not, in his view, the place for the enforcement of dogmas. Therefore, though Beatrice might have done better in life to win Count Francesco from his evil ways by peace and love, a theatre audience would yawn at his conversion; the real themes of the case—revenge, retaliation, and atonement—were also the fabric of effective drama.

Holding these opinions on the function of drama, Shelley set out to focus his play on the clash of passionate human beings. Although his treatment of the case is consequently less ideological than some of the modern settings, images repeatedly used by the poet highlight themes of the inadequacy of human justice and the struggle of youth with old age and authority. These two themes are combined in Cardinal Camillo's quotation of the Pope's explanation of unwillingness to punish Francesco for an impious celebration of the death of two sons:

> In the great war between the old and young
> I, who have white hairs and a tottering body,
> Will keep at least blameless neutrality.
> (act 2, scene 2, lines 38–40)

In Shelley's version, Beatrice and her co-conspirators are selfishly urged on by the young priest Orsino (the poet's name for the historical Monsignore Guerra) in the hope that the murder will put Beatrice and the family fortune in his power. Beatrice, however, dominates the play. After her father's crime against her (which gains in horror by never being expressly named), Shelley's heroine moves successively from a sense of degradation to a desire for self-purification, revenge, declaration of moral innocence, and resigned preparation for death.

Shelley's version has often been copied, but perhaps the greatest tribute came from his countryman, Walter Savage Landor, who loved Shelley's play so much that he declined to invite comparison between *The Cenci* and his own more modest work on the same theme. In his *Five Scenes* (1851), Landor wrote not a drama but five separate tableaux from the Cenci history, none of which portrayed either the act of incest or the murder. Landor's Beatrice is at once more girlish and more resolute than Shelley's heroine.

Another English poet who responded to the appeal of Beatrice and her fate was Robert Browning; the Cenci case has both historical and literary bonds with Browning's *The Ring and the Book*. In the Guido Franceschini case (on which Browning based his poem), defense counsel, in seeking to justify Guido's having avenged his honor after passage of time rather than in hot blood, was faced with the precedent of the conviction of Beatrice Cenci. He tried to avoid the force of this earlier case by quoting the explanation Beatrice's lawyer Farinaccio had given for his failure to obtain an acquittal: it was not that Beatrice had plotted revenge in cold blood, but that the incest charge had not been established. Wholly apart from this link in legal history, Browning acknowledged that *The Ring and the Book* owed an enormous literary debt to Shelley's *The Cenci*. In 1876, as a graceful token of gratitude, he addressed to Shelley's memory a short narrative poem, "Cenciaja," recounting the murder trial of Paolo Santacroce, the case that had influenced the refusal of Pope Clement VIII to grant clemency to Beatrice. According to Browning, the wrong Santacroce brother was executed for the crime.

The Cenci case also fascinated French writers. Stendhal was an avid collector of manuscripts of old Italian crimes. In 1837 he published a close rendering of a variant of the account of the Cenci case that provided the basis for the Shelley play. His most important literary contribution was a preface in which he presented Francesco as a corrupt mutation of what he called the Don Giovanni model. In Stendhal's concept the Don Giovanni type begins by expressing opposition to what he regards as the irrational conventions of a hypocritical society. In his decadent stage, illustrated by Francesco, Don Giovanni derives his pleasure from criminal excesses banned by reasonable social restrictions.

Two years after the Stendhal work, Alexandre Dumas the Elder contributed to a series of *Celebrated Crimes* an account of the Cenci case that draws on a source similar to Stendhal's and in some respects appears to plagiarize Stendhal's preface. However, Dumas shows none of Stendhal's reticence in dealing with the more lurid aspects of the case. Dumas' detailed account of the torture methods used even drew a complaint from Thackeray, who was himself a writer much concerned with crime and punishment.

In Italy the Cenci theme was seized upon by nineteenth-century men of letters who were associated with patriotic activity and anticlericalism. The dramatist Giovanni Battista Niccolini, an ardent republican and opponent of Church authority, made an unsuccessful adaptation of the Shelley play in 1838. Much more popular was the 1851 novel, *Beatrice Cenci*, by Francesco Domenico Guerrazzi, a patriot of the Risorgimento and an enemy of the Papal Government of Rome. Guerrazzi's account distorts the facts of the case beyond recognition. In his novel Beatrice is free of any guilt. Her father is murdered by her suitor Guerra, who surprises the count in the act of assaulting her. Beatrice is idealized in the extreme: she is a militant saint who, while defending her brothers and her honor, continually exhorts her father to repentance. Guerrazzi presents Francesco as a conscious believer in a doctrine of evil, who holds that man is free to commit any outrages until checked by divine intervention.

Beginning with the latter half of the nineteenth century, research in official archives has stripped away many of the Cenci legends and has given us a more humanized portrait of Beatrice. In 1877 Antonio Bertolotti published for the first time the text of a second codicil to Beatrice's will in which she made provision for a little boy, whom Bertolotti assumed to be a child born of her liaison with the murderer Olimpio. Bertolotti also believed that the alleged incest, to which Beatrice had never testified, was an invention of Farinaccio, whom Bertolotti denigrated as a man whose own loose morals had inspired the defense. Although Corrado Ricci, in his definitive study of the case in 1923, concurs in Bertolotti's conclusions with respect to the birth of Beatrice's child and the insubstantiality of the incest claim, he rejects Bertolotti's ridiculous attempt to rehabilitate Francesco as a man of religious conviction and leaves us a well-balanced view of Beatrice as a victim not free of fault but entitled to clemency, if not acquittal. Unfortunately, we must also credit to Ricci the definitive disproof of the charming tradition that Guido Reni's portrait of a sweet turbaned girl which until recent times hung in the Barberini Gallery is a death-cell painting of Beatrice. (This painting has been worshipped as an icon of Beatrice by throngs of literary tourists, including Shelley and Hawthorne, who devotes to the Reni work an entire chapter of *The Marble Faun*.) Ricci's version of the historical facts of the case provides the basis for many of the modern literary reconstructions that have followed, including the colorful novel of Frederic Prokosch, *A Tale for Midnight* (1955).

In the modern era, Antonin Artaud and Alberto Moravia have written dramas on the Cenci case that in quite different ways remove the conflict between Francesco and Beatrice from the plane of morality. Artaud's *The Cenci* (1935) was written and performed, with the author in the role of Francesco, as an approach towards realization of Artaud's concept of the Theatre of Cruelty. In Artaud's drama, sound, light, and gesture supplement the word in rousing the audience's responses. Artaud follows the narrative plan of Shelley's play, but there the similarity of the two works ends. Elements of myth, storm, and dream propel Artaud's drama, and the characters are forces of nature more than rational beings. Francesco is presented as personifying the myth of the "father-destroyer." Beatrice is not the embodiment of purity, but a force that is compelled to react to her father's violence. As her death approaches, Beatrice's principal fear is that she has come to resemble her father.

In Moravia's *Beatrice Cenci* (published in Italy in 1958), the ultimate kinship of the personalities of Francesco and Beatrice is also suggested. As in much of Moravia's work, all the characters are locked in their own worlds of isolation and egoism. Olimpio kills to maintain power over Beatrice, and Marzio kills for money. Francesco's crimes are explained by his weak sense of his own reality except when stimulated by excess. Beatrice explains her revenge not by an incestuous attack but by a childhood "loss of innocence" caused by witnessing an amorous passage of her father. However, Francesco charges that the root of her antagonism and of her failure to leave the castle of La Petrella is a trait she has inherited from him, an "incapacity for living."

The Cenci tragedy, with its mingling of pity and terror, seems as well suited to the opera stage as to the criminal courts. The history of its operatic treatments confirms the strong international appeal of the case and of its heroine. Appropriately, it was an Italian composer, Guiseppe Rota (1836–1903), who made the earliest operatic setting of which record survives. Rota's three-act tragedy, *Beatrice Cenci*, was first performed in 1863 in Rome. Subsequent operatic settings of the Cenci case have been composed and performed far from the home of the historical case. In 1927, *Beatrice Cenci*, an opera of the Polish composer Ludomir Rozycki had its premiere in Warsaw. This opera proved to be one of Rozycki's most popular works, and was revived in Poznan in 1936. The libretto, written by the composer and his wife, was based on a drama by Julius Słowacki, one of the most important Polish Romantics. Słowacki began his play in French in 1832 while he was in Paris and completed it in Polish in 1839 after his return to Paris. Considered as diverging from the Shelley treatment and antedating Stendhal in its original conception, Słowacki's work has been described as "pathetic, violent, full of a romantic splendor of style."

Supposed portrait of Beatrice Cenci attributed to Guido Reni.

A third version of the opera, *Beatrice Cenci*, by Berthold Gold-schmidt, a German-born composer and conductor residing in England, was awarded a Festival of Britain prize in 1951. In 1953 BBC broadcast excerpts from the opera conducted by the composer with the London Philharmonic Orchestra. The libretto for the opera, which followed the

Shelley text verbatim to the extent possible, was prepared by the composer in collaboration with drama critic Martin Esslin. Certain poems of Shelley, such as "Unfathomable Sea," were also included in the libretto.

Albert Ginastera's *Beatrix Cenci* reflects, as did its predecessor, *Bomarzo*, the composer's predilection for the violent history of the Italian Renaissance. The libretto, which was written in Spanish by William Shand, an Englishman residing in Argentina, and the poet Alberto Girri, is based on the Shelley play. As in Shelley's drama, the Ginastera work preserves the incestuous rape as the crucial act of violence begetting the tragedy. However, both the libretto and the concept of the production appear to bring the Ginastera opera closer to the spirit of Artaud than to the nineteenth-century precursors. Projections of slides and movies, dream sequences, and dramatic lighting effects are used and, fulfilling Artaud's requirement that each character have his own "particular cry," the climactic end of the first act is dominated by the barking of the count's mastiffs and Beatrice's prolonged scream of anguish.

The Ginastera opera, like the Artaud and Moravia plays, is informed by the vision that this old Renaissance tragedy can speak to us still of the violence of our own era, a violence that can overcome the comfort of the family and the promise of youth. Thus the chorus in the opening scene calls Count Cenci "a forerunner of our own times." This understanding of the continuing relevance of the case must also be conceded to the earlier masters of the Cenci story. In fact, one of the Cencis' judges in act 5, scene 1 of Shelley's tragedy makes a comment on the murder evidence that may serve to explain why the awful facts of the case have universal meaning. The judge says of the testimony: "This sounds as bad as truth."

Innocence and Arsenic:
The Literary and Criminal
Careers of C. J. L. Almquist

Two things are white—innocence and arsenic.
C. J. L. Almquist, The Queen's Jewel

Oscar Wilde's article "Pen, Pencil and Poison" (1889) is the first important essay on the artist as criminal. In this piece, Wilde reviewed the career of Thomas Griffiths Wainewright as poet, painter, art-critic—and poisoner. From his study of Wainewright's life, Wilde drew a characteristic conclusion: "The fact of a man being a poisoner is nothing against his prose."

With all due respect to the accomplishments of Wainewright in the varied fields of his endeavor, his case must be judged a poor second to that of the brilliant Swedish writer and "Renaissance man," Carl Jonas Love Almquist. Almquist, who was born in 1793 and died in 1866, was a novelist, poet, dramatist, essayist, composer and musical theoretician, civil servant, educator, clergyman, journalist, and religious and social reformer. His career ended in fifteen years of disgrace and exile, after he fled Sweden to escape charges of theft, fraud, and attempted arsenic poisoning. The lasting significance of Almquist's varied literary and intellectual activities justifies our putting him far ahead of Wainewright in the list of artist-criminals. He was one of the leading European writers in the second quarter of the nineteenth century and has been called, according to the *Columbia Encyclopedia*, "the only Swedish novelist of genius in the period 1830–1850." His work is in the mainstream of European Romanticism, showing strong affinities to Goethe, Friedrich

Schlegel, Victor Hugo, and Sir Walter Scott. Only because he wrote in the Swedish language and few of his books have been translated has he been denied the international readership his best work deserves. Although he had no professional training as a musician and his music is little known abroad, Almquist also was a talented song composer and his musical career receives a respectful summary in *Grove's Dictionary*.

In Sweden Almquist's name remains a household word. His novella *It Will Do* is still studied in secondary schools as an example of early realism, and his two principal romantic novels, *Amorina* and *The Queen's Jewel*, were given successful dramatic presentations in the 1950s. His music has been arranged and imitated by modern Swedish composers, and the international opera star Elisabeth Söderstrom uses Almquist's songs as her personal trademark in recital programs.

In addition to Almquist's permanent creative achievements, we find in his case a feature that makes it of greater criminological interest than that of Wainewright: throughout his life, Almquist was fascinated by the study of crime, criminal responsibility, and penology. The comic purpose of Wilde's linkage of Wainewright's artistic and criminal careers was to demonstrate a typical Wildean paradox—that art is amoral and that murder can be aesthetic. However, a study of Almquist's literary career and its criminal aftermath, though certainly not devoid of comedy, leaves room for more serious speculation about the relationship between intellectual activity and criminal impulses. Many of the ideas about death, crime, and personality that developed and recurred in his literary work later seemed to cast a sinister light on Almquist's own code of conduct when he stood charged with serious crimes.

Almquist came from a family of scholars, clergymen, and civil servants. His father Carl Gustav apparently was a practical businessman with little inclination for literature or aesthetics. It is hard to conceive of a more oddly matched couple than Carl Gustav and his wife, Brite-Louise. She was brought up in the religion of the Moravian Brotherhood by her father; with his support she fostered in the young Almquist a great and permanent affinity for the introspective religious feelings of the Moravians, to which he later gave a highly personal expression in his short lyrical poems, the *Songes*. Brite-Louise's devotion to nature was reinforced by her reading of Rousseau. Her son was to write of her that she loved nothing better than to daydream in the woods, "either alone or with Rousseau."

Almquist detected a duality in his own personality which he attributed to split inheritances from his father and mother. He said that he had two souls—the soul of a clerk, inherited from his father, and the soul of a

C. J. L. Almquist.

poet, with which his mother had endowed him. Whether or not Almquist had correctly defined the source of the elements of his character, there is no doubt that in his literary work and his own life there constantly recurs the theme of multiplexity and fluidity of personality. The most striking example in his novels is the androgynous Tintomara, one of the principal characters in his novel, *The Queen's Jewel*. Tintomara represents not the bisexual but rather the Platonic unification (and neutralization) of the male and female. She is the complete being free of the emotional and sexual cravings of the male or female. Tintomara also symbolizes the transcendence of the human soul by what Almquist referred to as the "celestial animal" soul, a soul that moves in graceful accord with the rhythm of nature and is indifferent to considerations of convention and morality. It is tempting to relate to Almquist's preoccupation with duality and change in personality his delight (no doubt also partly linguistic and antiquarian in origin) with the alteration of names as an emblem of shifts in identity. Thus, the chimerical Tintomara was never baptized. She is identified first merely as "She" and then as "the girl." In subsequent pages of *The Queen's Jewel*, she bears a bewildering succession of names, "Azouras," "Lazuli," "Tintomara," "Tourne-rose." The last name is particularly significant since it is a gallicized form of the name of the fourteen-volume work in which the bulk of Almquist's writings appeared, the *Book of the Briar Rose*. This collection is itself a mirror of multiplexity and change in literary expression and form: its poems, essays, and dramatic and narrative forms jangle against each other, often within the same work, creating the impression of what Almquist was to call a "fugue." Thus, the changeable and amoral Tintomara was consciously taken by Almquist as the symbol of his own work.

The heroine of Almquist's drama-novel *Amorina* is first known as Henrika, but her name changes to Amorina when she becomes a religious pilgrim. Here again, Almquist makes a strenuous effort to associate the heroine's name with the author. The name Amorina linguistically suggests the Latin word for "love," *amor*, and this association is appropriate to the heroine in her role as preacher of the gospel of love. But the name also is linked to the name of the fictional author of the work, who is identified in the introduction as Andreas Morin Anderson. This imaginary author rather oddly was accustomed to substitute initials for his first and last names; thus he was A. Morin A., which is a cryptogram for the name of his heroine. It will also be recalled that Almquist's third Christian name was "Love" (pronounced Loo-vuh in Swedish). Surely, no more elaborate linguistic trick has ever been played to identify an author with his character.

Were these changeable fictional creatures with the kaleidoscopic names also the symbol of Almquist's life? It is remarkable how often a change in name is associated with critical junctures in his life. The first was his change of his name to Love Carlsson when he decided in 1824 to live the life of a Rousseauist peasant and to marry a peasant girl. An equally dramatic instance was the later charge that he had been guilty of counterfeiting (the crime most closely resembling the craft of the writer, according to Gide) through alteration of his name on promissory notes.

Almquist's mother died in 1806, when he was only twelve. That this loss had a strong impact on Almquist we have from his own words, but he apparently made an effort to suppress any outward display of his grief. It is, of course, risky to attempt to assay the effect of this early loss of love on his later development, but some have related this trauma to his lack of success in marriage. Since other diurnal problems may intervene in these matters (such as poor housekeeping, of which he accused his peasant wife), it is perhaps safer to follow the traces in his literary work. Here we find that the death of a mother often plays an important role—the death of the mother of the Löwenstjerna children in *The Hunting Lodge*, the death of Henrika's mother in *Amorina*, the death of Tintomara's mother in *The Queen's Jewel*.

Perhaps more significant is the death of Sara Videbeck's mother in *It Will Do*. Almquist wrote this novella to illustrate the viability of "free marriage," which he also advocated in his essays and tracts, that is, a relationship of man and woman, unblessed by clergy, dissoluble at will, and without sharing of property (or even of permanent living quarters). Almquist's marriage theories were to find their fullest development in his reformist work, *The Grounds of European Discontent*, published around the same time as *It Will Do*, in which he argued that children should belong to the woman alone and that child support payments should be provided from a children's insurance fund.

The novella *It Will Do* describes the origin of a free marriage between Sara Videbeck and a young sergeant named Albert, whom she meets by chance on a boat journey. During the voyage it appears that the couple have become lovers but the physical side of their relationship is not completely clear, for Sara spends most of her time elucidating Almquist's marriage theories. In fact, one begins to feel that poor Albert may have fallen in love with Almquist in female disguise. However, the emotional tone of the book changes at the end, when Sara returns home several days late because of detours taken with Albert and learns of the death of her mother, who had long been ill. The expression of her grief at her mother's burial far surpasses any tokens of love that she had bestowed on Albert during their voyage, and it may be that there is also more than a tinge of guilt that the romantic voyage had been responsible for her not being with her mother during her last hours.

During his early years Almquist came under the influence of Sweden-borgian teachings, an influence that was to continue to be felt strongly in his life and writings. He was particularly affected by the Swedenborgian belief that the earthly life was an experimental preparation for a personal life in eternity; that earthly marriage was a reflection of the celestial marriage of truth and beauty. Although, as noted before, Almquist was also attracted by the Moravians' inwardness, he did not follow them in their indifference to dogma, but instead, to his eventual downfall, followed the Swedenborgians in their aggressive assault on established church doctrine.

All of the intellectual influences we have noted—his mother's Rousseauist preference for the countryside and nature, his grandfather's Moravianism, and his own interest in Swedenborgian doctrine—are joined together in shaping Almquist's doctrine of love which underlies his marriage theory and much of his fiction and poetry as well. This doctrine was expounded in his first published work, *What is Love?*, which appeared in 1819. In this essay he argued that genuine love is found only in the truly religious and arises out of emotion. This concept of love had nothing to do with conventional morality. In *What is Love?* we hear the first expression of his opposition to contractual, religiously sanctioned marriage. Wedlock to him was immoral except when sanctioned by love. The man who falsified a vow of love in a wedding ceremony was, in his view, far worse than a counterfeiter of notes. He wrote:

> The law hangs the forger of notes, no doubt rightly for the public good, but he who falsifies love, that is, he who for a thousand reasons other than love unites with a person whom he does not love and thereby creates an evil domestic circle, does not he commit a crime the magnitude of which and incalculable consequences of which, both present and future, occasion much more terrible misfortune than does the forging of millions of notes?

The counterfeiter with love in his heart was less of a social evil than the bad husband with ready cash. Thirty-odd years later, however, it was Almquist himself who was charged with falsifying notes, and the Swedish court had not been convinced by Almquist's writings that the quality of his feelings had any bearing on the case.

Another characteristic of Almquist's career and work is the constant alternation between fantasy and realism. He was able to function brilliantly in either realm. During the period when he was penning some of the most bizarre books in Swedish literature he was also serving quite ably (between 1825 and 1840) as a teacher at the New Elementary School in Stockholm, where he turned out a number of respected textbooks, including Swedish, Greek and French grammars, a famous Swedish orthography, a beginners' arithmetic text and a general world history. The wildest romanticism inspired his organizational program, published in 1820, for the short-lived Manhem Society, a proposal to reeducate the Swedish people in defined stages up from their origins in Nordic myth through medieval Christianity to the final form of an idealized peasantry uniting love of God with love of the Swedish land. And seventeen years later, despite his public differences with the religious establishment, he found it possible to become ordained as a regular Lutheran clergyman. He could write a piece of political satire in the form of science fiction, in which the ultimate power resided in a well-meaning but misguided divinity headquartered on the moon. Later he was capable of dealing with politics in practical terms as a contributor to the radical newspaper, the *Aftonbladet*. But as in the pages of his literary "fugues" the reader is wrenched without warning from realistically portrayed scenes to the wildest shores of fantasy, so in his life the borders of imagination and reality sometimes became blurred. Thus, the attempt of Almquist to carry out the life of the idealized peasant lasted only about a year, and his selection of a peasant girl for his wife doomed him to an unhappy marriage. He is said to have been happy with his wife only when he was away from her and his imagination could go to work again.

In his private relations, too, we see the signs of a personality frequently passing between fantasy and fact. It was observed that there was in the man a love of mystification for its own sake. He would regale his friends and acquaintances with outrageous fabrications to no apparent purpose except creative enjoyment. His son, at the time of Almquist's legal difficulties, was to write that Almquist had the ability to come to believe firmly in his own inventions.

Throughout his career, both in his fiction and in his essays and journalism, Almquist showed a keen interest in crime. One of his earliest works (published around 1820) is a treatise on the treatment of criminals, in which, without attempting to resolve the question of freedom of will, he concludes that the criminal is to be regarded as sick. The purposes of treatment of the criminal should be rehabilitation, and, if he is incorrigible, he should be separated from society to prevent him from doing further harm. This theme is echoed in his later novel, *Three Wives in Småland*, which appeared in 1842–43. Here Almquist's advocacy of the penal colony as an appropriate mode of punishment is given a Kafkaesque religious basis by one of the characters in the novel, who observes that, since the fall of Man, the whole world is a penal colony.

In addition to his theoretical interest in crime, it is known that while in Paris in 1840 Almquist mentioned in letters to the *Aftonbladet* the famous arsenic poisoning trial of Marie Lafarge, which was then proceeding in a small French town. Later, he was to write an article for the

Aftonbladet comparing the Lafarge case with a sensational Swedish arsenic poisoning case, the Attarp murder.

Almquist's treatment of murder in his novels raises certain disturbing questions in light of his subsequent history. One wonders whether his Swedenborgian belief in the afterlife and the tentative quality of earthly existence made him rank murder (as he had rated counterfeiting) relatively low on the scale of crime when compared with what he proclaimed to be the greatest sin, the failure to love. In Almquist's prose epic *Murnis*, the spirit of a man named Albion unhappily confesses to a group of angels in heaven that while on earth Albion has accidentally caused the death of his best beloved. The angels reply: "Have you murdered your best beloved? Then you have murdered her unto life." In *The Hunting Lodge*, Richard Furumo, a poet reminiscent of Almquist himself, pushes Magdalena over a cliff at just the moment in which she is filled with religious ecstasy. His action is a criminal application of the Swedenborgian idea that a person wakes up to the new life in the same spiritual state in which he departed the earthly life. Almquist was himself later accused of having caused the death of a young couple in a suicide pact by the inculcation of his Swedenborgian views.

It is also striking that Almquist's fiction tends to displace responsibility for murder from the murderer to outside influences—inheritance, society or nature. Thus, in *Amorina* (written in 1822 and published in 1839), the crimes of Johannes, a mass murderer, are attributed to an inherited bloodlust, to misuse of his criminal tendencies by corrupt nobles, and to rejection of his demand for absolution by a materialistic clergyman. Strangely enough, we end up sympathizing with him, much as we sympathize with King Kong as the fighter planes close in. Tintomara in *The Queen's Jewel* (1834) is completely indifferent to the fact that she was used by the assassins of King Gustave III to lure him to death at the famous masked ball celebrated by Verdi. To her, as a "celestial animal," all death is a part of nature. When she is asked whether she has seen how it looks when a person dies, she replies: "My mother died and I saw it." Again, the theme of the death of a mother. Can Almquist's early loss have paradoxically prepared the way both for his ready acceptance of Swedenborgian belief in the afterlife—and the underestimation of the significance of murder?

Hugo Hamilcar Löwenstjerna, one of the principal characters of the *Book of the Briar Rose*, claims in *Academic Thoughts*, published together with the novel *Three Wives in Småland*, to have penetrated "the mystery of crime." He maintains that it is "through crime that humanity progresses, and each new stage of development consists of the foremost mortal sin that the preceding form of social development most of all forbad and with all its might, its wisdom, and its legislation sought to prevent." Hugo proceeds to explain that each society considers as the most dangerous crimes such actions as would tend to break down the structure of existing society and prepare the way for the next stage of development. When asked whether there were not also acts that were perpetually crimes against God, regardless of the stage of social development, Hugo replies, in Almquist's familiar formula, that the greatest crime against God was "not to love everyone and everything."

But as novelist, if not as theorist, Almquist doubtless recognized that, despite Hugo's dictum, the mystery of crime is impenetrable. At least at times he must have recognized the ambiguity that marks not only external evidence of guilt and innocence but also the nature and origin of crime and the criminal impulse. Certainly, some of this ambiguity is expressed in the famous paradox that Tintomara's mother leaves her as a final bequest in a dramatic scene in *The Queen's Jewel*: "Tintomara," she cries, "two things are white: innocence and arsenic."

From 1841 on, Almquist's fortunes deteriorated. After public controversy over the publication of his fictional tract on free marriage, *It Will Do*, he was dismissed from his position with the New Elementary School and had to attempt to support himself with his journalistic work and his small income as a regimental chaplain. It is at this point that his literary career ends, and his career as a suspected criminal begins.

In early June 1851, rumors began to spread that indicated he might have been supplementing his income by defrauding elderly ex-Captain Johan Jacob von Scheven. Von Scheven was an eccentric and miserly recluse who tried to support himself by usury. But he made profits on paper and losses in fact because of his excessive credulity and because he was more interested in high interest than the reliability of the borrower. Almquist had been on close terms with von Scheven, and served him in some of his business dealings as well as sharing cultural interests. It was rumored that Almquist had stolen from the old man a number of promissory notes that had been signed by Almquist to evidence substantial personal borrowings. It was also said that, in order to avoid discovery of his theft, Almquist had attempted to poison the captain. The belief in the rumors was strengthened by Almquist's flight from Sweden before his arrest could be effected.

The charges with respect to both the notes and the poisoning attempt were put before a military court that had jurisdiction over Almquist as a regimental chaplain. Under Swedish law at that time attempted poisoning was a capital offense and the court had authority to pass judgment on Almquist despite his absence, since he was a fugitive from justice. However, the court, while making a finding of probable guilt on all

counts, merely deferred the matter for further consideration and contented itself with stripping Almquist of his post as chaplain. Later, a
bankruptcy court, on the petition of the understandably annoyed Captain von Scheven, sentenced Almquist in absentia to be pilloried and
imprisoned as an embezzler.

The evidence at the trial (considered at length by A. Hemming-
Sjöberg in *A Poet's Tragedy*, which appeared in English translation in
1932) reads like a plot from one of Almquist's novels, but certainly not
from his best period—more like one of the thrillers of his last period
which he wrote in the French style. The first event in the strange case was
a mysterious disappearance (around May 31, 1851) of the bearer notes
that Almquist had issued to Captain von Scheven. The captain prodded
Almquist to replace them with new notes and Almquist finally did so on
June 3. The substitution of the notes was accomplished in a manner
worthy of the comic artist. Almquist signed the new notes in a hand so
faint that the feeble-sighted captain protested he could not read them.
Yielding to the captain's complaints, Almquist rewrote the notes but
placed them in a closed envelope. The next day von Scheven's good
friend and landlord, Alderman Lorentz, examined the notes and pointed out that they were signed "Alm*gren*." The novelist, on being confronted with this variation of his surname, protested that this was his
usual manner of signing, but he changed the final letters to a more regular "quist." However, what the eyes of captain and friends did not catch
was that Almquist had sealed the new notes with a seal that he did not
customarily use.

The purpose of all this was apparently to prepare the way for a claim,
on presentation of the notes for payment, that they were not genuine.
But how much more convenient to make such a claim to representatives
of Captain von Scheven's estate than to the captain, who could testify as
to the original loan and the circumstances of the substitution of the
notes? For this to be possible, of course, the captain had to die before the
collection effort began in earnest.

The evidence with respect to the poisoning charge was that Almquist
had put arsenic into the von Scheven's brandy bottle and also mixed it
with his gruel. The transactions relating to the substitution and signing
of the promissory notes were punctuated by unhappy encounters (or
near-misses) between the captain and his gruel. The first gruel episode,
which set the pattern for others, went like this: on Sunday, June 1, after
discovery of the disappearance of the original notes and the requests to
Almquist for new notes, the captain felt unwell and ordered some gruel
from his servant, Hedda. Almquist arrived at this point, and when von
Scheven renewed his request for new notes, Almquist offered to slip into

the kitchen to see how the gruel was coming along. Hedda testified at the trial that Almquist had sent her out of the kitchen to fetch him the bathroom key. He was now alone with the gruel. When Hedda returned she noticed some white grains floating on the surface of the gruel. At Hedda's suggestion, the captain threw the stuff away, but more whitish gruel was served up to him two days later. On Saturday, June 7, when the captain, by now understandably in need of a stiff drink, poured himself some brandy, the sharp-eyed Hedda observed "that the brandy was cloudy and that several white grains had lain in the bottom of the bottle."

And so Almquist's life, which had resounded so often to the themes of his writing, was to center now on the determination of the quality of a white substance in the gruel and the brandy. Was this white substance innocent or was it arsenic? The chemists said arsenic.

There was also testimony indicating that Almquist had tried to obtain poisons other than arsenic, which, he knew from his familiarity with the Lafarge and Attarp cases, was easy to trace. Here, the hand of the artist appears. Most classic poisoners of the nineteenth century acquired poisons for the avowed purpose of improving their complexions or killing rats, but Almquist, in asking a chemist for the poison *nux vomica*, explained that he wanted to see what it looked like, so that he could describe it in a novel he was working on.

There is also evidence of energetic efforts to plant clues pointing the finger of guilt in every possible direction. He had a problem here. The first suspects in a domestic crime are usually the close relatives. But Captain von Scheven was alienated from his wife and son. Almquist apparently made an attempt to reconcile them with the captain shortly before the poisoning attempts began. He also attempted to throw suspicion on a young girl who was living in von Scheven's home (under equivocal circumstances) by sending her an anonymous letter urging her to flee. And then, for good measure, he left room for the possibility of a suicide by claiming to have found a lump of arsenic behind a book in the captain's bookcase. In fact, the police *did* find a lump of arsenic in the bookcase—right behind a volume of Swedenborg that Almquist was fond of reading to the captain.

The poisoning attempts failed, and Almquist made a dash for abroad, after pretending to von Scheven (who was pressing for payment) and to his family and friends that he was leaving on a brief trip. On his way out of the country, he added another name alteration to his skein, changing his initials on his first passport application.

Unfortunately, in his haste he left behind several memoranda setting forth in detail the factual and legal arguments he would make in the face of criminal charges. Almquist claimed from overseas that the memo-randa were prepared after the rumors of his crimes arose and not in advance. Particularly damning, however, were references in the memo-randa to the arguments which he would make to contest the existence of any debt to von Scheven in the event of the captain's death.

In his letters from abroad Almquist indicated that it was his intention to praise the captain, not to bury him. But the praise was decidedly faint. He wrote: "as on one occasion he rendered me considerable monetary assistance without usury (for which he was otherwise notorious), I con-ceived a certain attachment to him and considered him much better than most people's judgment of him." And he added in another letter: "Why should I hate the old man, who, though he certainly was unpleasant on various occasions and is unwilling to wash himself, yet cannot possibly be the object of hatred on that account?" This was the practical applica-tion of Almquist's doctrines of love.

Almquist lived abroad for fifteen years after his flight from Sweden. His escape route took him through Denmark, Germany, and England to the United States. He stopped in St. Louis, New Orleans, and Texas, and lived in Cincinnati in 1853 and 1854. He finally settled in Philadelphia, where he lived from 1854 until 1865. Then, driven by homesickness, he left for Bremen, Germany, where he died the following year.

Posthumous study of the final years of Almquist's life has yielded suggestive evidence of the persistence of certain personal traits with which we have already become familiar. There is first that curious preoccupation with the alteration of names, as, Zorba-like, he wandered through the United States, first as Abraham Jacobson, and then as Lewis Gustawi. During his last days in Bremen he was successively known as Professor Jules Charles and then as the presumably equally scholarly Professor Carl Westermann. In Philadelphia, while he was still Lewis Gustawi, he entered a bigamous marriage with his landlady, Emma Nugent, apparently obtaining his amatory success on the basis of his misrepresentations that he was a wealthy man. Again, as in the von Scheven case, he found refuge from his crime in literature, preparing a memorandum setting forth the defense he would make to the charge that the marriage was fraudulently induced. He wrote that he did not tell Emma that he possessed property, but rather that he had an expectation of the receipt of property. His defense against the charge that these great expectations were also imaginary presumably was deferred for a later memorandum which was never written.

His powers of imagination remained unimpaired, if we may judge by a Münchhausen-like letter which he wrote describing his personal at-tendance as spectator at the Battle of Gettysburg. He claims to have retrieved as a souvenir of the battle the hat of one of his best friends who evidently had a less favorable spot along the sidelines and, according to Almquist, fell "in one of the hottest melees."

It is a matter of speculation whether Almquist ever recognized himself as a criminal. It is ironic to note that if this recognition ever came to him, he had meted out to himself through his exile the punishment that his penological theory accorded to incorrigible criminals—separation from the society of his fellow-citizens.

However, research has never uncovered any evidence of a confession by Almquist of any of the criminal charges against him. In fact, his own final estimate of his life may have been that he had in all respects complied with the following credo which he avowed in a poem he wrote shortly before his death:

> I will . . . never do the slightest harm
> to the smallest creature in the world.

Strict Construction in Sung China: The Case of A Yün

History is often made by minor wounds. The report that an English shipmaster named Jenkins had had an ear cut off by Spanish coast guards led to war between England and Spain in 1739. In Sung China of the eleventh century a young man's loss of a finger in an assault by his fiancée, A Yün, gave rise to a legal *cause célèbre* that preoccupied the imperial court and helped to make or break the careers of some of the empire's principal officials.

It is always interesting to trace the growth of major public controversy from small beginnings, but the case of A Yün yields more than narrative rewards. Complementing the broad studies Prof. Jerome Alan Cohen and others have made of Chinese Communist criminal procedure, the study of traditional criminal cases, such as that of A Yün, teaches us to be cautious before attributing to Communist innovation attitudes that may have their roots much deeper in the Chinese past. These attitudes include an ambivalence toward the societal role of law and emphasis on the importance of "confession." Detailed case studies of imperial criminal trials may lead us to re-examine or qualify many of the generalizations that have been made about traditional Chinese concepts of criminal law—for example, the assumption that principles of technical statutory construction excluded more pragmatic considerations such as clemency and deterrence of criminal conduct.

A short summary of the philosophical approach of Chinese tradition to criminal law will set the stage for A Yün's celebrated onslaught on Wei, her unfortunate betrothed. The Chinese attitude combined elements of idealism and realism—the idealistic vision of the Confucian "superior man" who is motivated by piety and good example, not by fear of the law, and the realistic view that a system of reasonable criminal sanctions is necessary for those who cannot meet minimum standards of social conduct. The coexistence of these two ideological strands is sometimes explained historically as the result of the "Confucianization" of the position of the Legalists, who believed that few men are naturally good and that the restraints of stern punishments are necessary. They influenced the adoption by the Ch'in court of a penal code that was applied to all China after the establishment of a national government by the Ch'in Dynasty in the late third century B.C. The idea of a penal code survived through the succeeding dynasties, but the Legalists' emphasis on universally fixed penalties came to be modified by Confucian concepts of humanism and social differentiation.

Long before the triumph of Legalism, however, the early Chinese classics, which Confucius admired and to which he is traditionally believed to have given final form, assigned a beneficent role to the appropriate application of criminal penalties. One of the earliest minister-heroes in the oldest complete Chinese classic that survives, *The Book of History*, is Kao Yao, a minister of crime in the third millennium B.C., whose intelligent and moderate application of the "five penalties" assisted in "the inculcation of the five cardinal duties" and in general law-abiding behavior that entails no punishment at all. The faith here expressed in the teaching function of "letting the punishment fit the crime"—that is, the belief that the degree of severity of the penalty defines with great precision the relative seriousness of the offense—survived throughout the history of Imperial China. Even the "five penalties" with successive modification and subdivision remained the core of a finely graded scale of penalties. In the Sung Dynasty the five penalties in descending order of severity were death, deportation, forced labor, beating with heavy rod, and beating with light rod. Each category of punishment was subdivided by degrees intended to match finely calibrated measures of criminal responsibility.

The differences between Imperial China and the West were as great in criminal procedure as in the ideological basis for punishment. There were no lawyers. The local magistrate combined the functions of detective, prosecutor, and judge. Evidence could be obtained under torture. The aversion the citizen must have felt to litigation appears to survive etymologically. In the common literary word for *lawsuit* under the empire, the character for *speech* appears between two variants of the character for *dog*. A trial apparently summoned up a scene of two dogs barking at each other. The principal protections of the criminal defendant were the restrictions placed on the magistrate by public opinion, severe criminal sanctions applied to judicial misconduct, and the availability of appeal through a number of levels that ascended in serious cases to the Ministry of Justice (Board of Punishments), one of the principal imperial ministries, and to the emperor himself.

The facts of A Yün's case have a deceptive simplicity when compared with the manifold legal issues they raised. A young girl by the name of A Yün was, while still mourning for her mother, betrothed to a man by the name of Wei. Betrothal during a period of mourning for a parent was itself a serious crime in China. Whether she was embarrassed by this impious act or whether Wei proved a bit of a cad we do not know, but in any event A Yün planned to get rid of him. She lay in wait for him in a field hut and struck him several times with a knife. She was not successful in killing him but did cut off one of his fingers. At first the local authorities investigating the attack considered the possibility of an attempted robbery, but eventually suspicion fell on A Yün. She was arrested and questioned by the local magistrate and confessed the crime after having been threatened with torture.

The case presented a number of issues under the Sung penal code, which had been carried over with only modest change from the code of the preceding T'ang Dynasty. A potentially dangerous issue was whether the victim could be regarded as A Yün's husband, since the murder of a husband was one of the most serious criminal offenses. For purposes of the criminal law, the couple was not regarded as married until the bride was, in the course of the wedding ceremony, introduced into the ancestral hall of her husband. Although this ceremony had not been accomplished and therefore Wei was not a husband under the criminal code, A Yün's defenders were to argue for good measure that in any event Wei could not be regarded as her husband since a betrothal during a period of mourning was to be regarded as a nullity.

A more crucial issue was the effect of A Yün's confession. The Chinese imperial codes placed great value on confession as reflecting moral and social benefits. From a moral standpoint confession represented a voluntary return of the defendant to the path of virtue. From the social point of view confession served to avoid the necessity of legal procedure, which in the Confucian system is considered less worthy than internalized moral standards as a means of controlling behavior.

The timing of a confession had an important effect on legal consequences. The Sung code provided that "when a criminal defendant, before his criminal deed has been disclosed, confesses, his punishment will be remitted." When the defendant makes his confession before the community is even aware of his crime, the voluntary nature of his confession is evident, with the result that he receives full immunity. A subsection of the same statutory provision further stated that a wrongdoer who confesses after a charge has been brought against him but before his interrogation is first "under contemplation" is not to be given a full remission of the penalty but only a moderation to the extent of two penalty degrees.

Under the circumstances covered by this subsection, it is not clear that the confessing defendant has sincerely repented, since the community already suspects him and he has been charged by the authorities, but his confession is still given a substantial reward since it is to some extent voluntary and serves the purpose of avoiding legal procedure. It was clear that A Yün did not qualify for a full remission of penalty since she was already under suspicion at the time of the confession. Under traditional interpretations, it is doubtful that she was even entitled to the benefit of the subsection providing for reduction of penalty since her confession was given only after interrogation began and when threat of further interrogation under torture had already been made.

Surprisingly little of the controversy in the A Yün case centered on the issue of the timeliness of the confession. The principal focus of contention was instead the applicability of an important statutory limitation on remission or reduction of penalties by reason of confession—that no mitigation was granted when the crime confessed had resulted in irreparable injury. The loss of Wei's finger was an irreparable injury. This mutilation, however, did not dispose of the legal question. The highly particularistic provisions on homicide in the Sung code defined a number of offenses in the nature of "felony murder." Under these provisions a killing or wounding was punished more severely than mere "intentional killing" (manslaughter) or "intentional wounding," if certain prohibited conduct had resulted in the injury, for example, killing in the course of resisting arrest or in connection with unlawful slavery.

These complex crimes were analyzed as consisting of two elements: (1) the act of injury and (2) the so-called causative crime, such as resisting arrest. The official commentary on the code, which had the force of law, provided: "Whoever is guilty of a killing or wounding and confesses, thereby is entitled to remission of the penalty for the causative crime; in such event, recourse will be had to the statutory provisions for intentional killing and wounding." Under this provision a confession of a felony murder could result, depending on the time it was made, in (1) complete remission of the felony murder penalty and prosecution for simple manslaughter or (2) reduction by two degrees of the penalty applicable to the felony murder.

A Yün's crime did not appear to lend itself easily to any division between injury and causative crime. She appeared to be guilty of a unitary crime—premeditated homicide resulting in injury, an offense subject to capital punishment. This was indeed the ruling of the local magistrate who first heard her case. The decision, however, aroused the keen interest of Hsü Tsun, a friend of the important imperial minister, Wang An-shih. Hsü argued strongly against the judgment in the case. He originated the theory that the crime with which A Yün was charged was a felony wounding, subject to division into two elements, the injury itself and a causative crime, that is, the planning of homicide that resulted in the injury. He argued that A Yün's confession entitled her to a reduction of two degrees in the penalty for planned homicide resulting in injury—and therefore brought into play the application of a form of penal servitude instead of capital punishment.

He argued his case so strongly that he was charged with the offense of litigiousness. Although he escaped punishment for his persistent advocacy, he was unable to have the High Court of Justice accept his view. Despite the fact that in the course of the appellate process the capital penalty had been commuted, apparently as a result of judicial clemency, Hsü Tsun continued to press for recognition of A Yün's statutory rights. Such a stir over the matter had been made in the capital that the Emperor Shen Tsung ordered two of the principal officials of the empire, Wang An-shih and Ssu-ma Kuang, to present to the throne their joint opinion.

It was a vain hope on the part of the emperor that these two statesmen would be able to reach agreement on anything, whether in the arena of politics or law. Ssu-ma Kuang, who was to become one of China's greatest historians, was a responsible Confucian conservative, with a strong respect for administrative and legal precedent and an ingrained suspicion of innovation. Wang An-shih, who had been called recently to the capital after long years of service in local and provincial administration, also regarded himself as an orthodox Confucian minister, but he had a marked penchant for radical reform, particularly in the area of finance and economics. He was also active in the advancement of the study of law, establishing a national law school and substituting an examination in law for some of the more formalistic subjects in the civil service examinations.

The A Yün case made its way to the capital during the very early stage (1069 A.D.) of the struggle between Ssu-ma Kuang and Wang An-shih for primacy in the emperor's favor. Wang An-shih was destined not only to have the ultimate victory in the A Yün case but shortly thereafter to win appointment as prime minister and to initiate a series of far-reaching reforms in financial administration, state trading, and grain supply regulation, which are known to Chinese history as the New Policies.

Ssu-ma Kuang and Wang An-shih presented opposing arguments to the emperor regarding A Yün's case. These brought into conflict the views of two men, who, despite their political opposition, had a high regard for each other's intellectual attainments. They both regarded themselves as legitimate heirs of Confucian teaching. Each also could have fairly regarded himself as an advocate of the doctrine of "strict construction." That doctrine for the imperial Chinese as for ourselves includes two opposing considerations often in delicate balance at best. According to *Black's Law Dictionary*, the first is that "the court will not extend punishment to cases not plainly within the language used"; the second, that criminal statutes "are to be fairly and reasonably construed, and will not be given such a narrow and strained construction as to exclude from their operation cases plainly within their scope."

Advocates emphasizing one of these elements more strongly than the other sometimes have claimed the exclusive title of "strict constructionist." A valuable lesson in the interplay between the two countervailing factors in the doctrine can be seen in the opposing briefs of Wang An-shih and Ssu-ma Kuang, with Wang emphasizing reasonable narrowness of construction and his opponent emphasizing reasonable construction in the light of precedent and the obligation not to exclude cases by strained interpretation.

Ssu-ma Kuang believed that the case did not merit the attention of the emperor or his ministers but should have been handled and decided "by officials of mediocre talent." The application of legal provisions and precedents was the duty of the regular judges, and princes and their chancellors were responsible only for the establishment of special principles not within the general legal norms. According to Ssu-ma Kuang, disputes and lawsuits could be resolved only in accord with the norms of morality. "What morality rejects," he wrote in a memorial to the emperor, "is seized upon by criminal punishment." He added:

> If Your Majesty wanted to attempt to consider the case of A Yün from the standpoint of morality, how could it be difficult to decide? Such acute and complicated issues as whether a planned homicide is one crime or two crimes or whether planning is a causative crime or not should be disputed by officials who are experienced in the interpretation of the legal text. Why should enlightened princes and wise ministers deal with such a matter? The discussions have lasted for over a year without the case coming to a conclusion, and the result is that the eternal rules which have been effective for a hundred generations are abandoned and an attack is made on the great Laws of the Three Volumes, that the good and upstanding have no hearing, and that the outcast and evil triumph. Does this not result from the fact that one is following only the twigs and the leaves of the law and neglecting the roots and the trunk?

In his brief on the substantive issues of the case, Ssu-ma Kuang emphasized legislative intent. He focused on the policy supporting the provision that a person guilty of a homicide or wounding in the course of a crime, if he confesses, obtains remission of the penalty for the causative crime and is prosecuted under the statutory provisions relating to intentional killing or wounding. According to Ssu-ma, the statutory concern was that when a man in the course of a theft or other crime originally did not have the intention of killing or wounding but, in the course of the execution of the criminal act, came to commit the killing or wounding, a judge might, in the absence of the special statute, follow the letter of the law and not permit a confession to moderate the applicable penalty. This moderation was permitted in the event of confession by remission or reduction of the penalty for the causative crime, such as theft.

To Ssu-ma Kuang, the possibility of moderation was wise lawmaking because the moral responsibility for a murder or wounding in the course of a crime fell somewhere between the heavier responsibility for premeditated murder and the lighter responsibility for killing in an affray. When a killing or wounding was committed as the result of another causative crime, the relief of confession was permitted for the causative crime and the killing or wounding was punished as "intentional" killing or wounding, which was subject to a penalty lighter than premeditated murder but more severe than killing or wounding in a fight.

Ssu-ma pointed out that Hsü Tsun's effort to separate planning from killing or wounding and to designate the act of planning as a causative crime was illogical and could lead to anomalous application of penalties:

> But now Hsü Tsun wants to separate planning and killing into two events. However, planned killing and intentional killing are both killings. If one considers planning and killing to be two things, then one must also consider intention and killing to be two things. If one plans and deliberates very calmly but undertakes no killing, what crime does he have to confess? The word "planning" is thus only meaningful in conjunction with the word "killing" and does not represent a special, causative crime. If one wanted to say that robbery, fighting and planning are all causative crimes, and consequently that the penal provisions for intentional killing should be applied in the event of a confession, then one who confesses a killing in a fight would be punished one degree more severely than if he had not confessed. The fact that the death sentence of A Yün was remitted is already a great act of mercy. Hsü Tsun's persistence in demanding in her behalf that a precedential case be made leads to the opening of the way for all wrongdoers and to the encouragement of robbers, murderers and evildoers and is not good doctrine.

Wang An-shih in his opposing brief supported the position of Hsü Tsun that planning, unlike intention, is a causative act that can be separated from the criminal element of killing and wounding and is therefore subject to remission or reduction of penalty as a result of confession. He wrote:

In the statute there are a whole series of provisions for killing and wounding crimes. There is the crime caused by planning, that caused by robbery or theft, that caused through slavery, and that through resistance to arresting officials. All these are causative crimes for killing and wounding. Only intentional killing and wounding have no further cause. Therefore, the statute provides that those guilty of a killing or wounding, who confess, avoid the penalty for the causative crime, but are punished in accordance with the statutory provisions for intentional killing and wounding.

Wang met Ssu-ma Kuang's argument that this analysis could lead to the imposition of heavier penalties for certain crimes in the event of confession. He argued that it was the intent of the statute that the provision for remission of causative crimes would be applied only if a lighter penalty resulted. Negligent killing or wounding, or killing or wounding in an affray, was therefore always punished in accordance with the original statutory penalties applicable to these crimes, since these original penalties were lighter than the penalties for intentional killing and wounding applied in cases in which a causative element, such as planning, is remitted by reason of confession.

Wang then turned to the question of the legal prerequisites for determining whether an element of a crime constituted a causative crime or was, instead, a part of the killing or wounding act itself. He noted that the law spoke of a "cause, but not of a separate cause," and added:

I cannot understand why the planning of a killing cannot be viewed as a causative crime for a killing or wounding. And if the Ministry of Justice says that planning is directed towards a killing and therefore can be no causative crime, so I might reply, that for the planning of the killing three years of penal servitude is prescribed, and if a wounding results, death through hanging, and if a killing results, death through beheading. Planned killing, accomplished wounding, and accomplished killing are thus three distinct penal provisions. . . . The High Court of Justice and the Ministry of Justice place in the same category planned killing, for which in accordance with the statute remission of the penalty through confession is available, and accomplished wounding for which in accordance with the statute remission of the penalty through confession is not available. It is clear that this transgresses the intention of the statute. I am thus of the opinion that A Yün must be sentenced for planned killing and accomplished wounding in the light of consideration of her confession when the interrogation had first been taken into contemplation; and that her sentence must be determined in accordance with the provisions with regard to planned killing, reduced by two degrees.

Wang also dealt with the argument that permission of reduction of penalties for planned killing resulting in wounding would encourage similar crimes. He replied that the regular officials charged with judging these crimes should hold to the statute permitting reduction of penalty and that any special circumstances could be dealt with by imperial decree. He said that if the regular judicial officials had the right to depart from the statute in their criminal judgment, "justice will be shattered, and men will no longer know where to put their hands and feet."

Two followers of Wang An-shih, Lu Kung-shu and Chien Kung-fu, filed a supplemental brief following the line of Wang's argument but adding a further point of interest. They contended that if the effect of confession were ruled out in the case of a planned killing, persons contemplating such a crime would not have any reason to hold back from carrying out the killing, since the death penalty would face them in any event. If one left such criminals with hope, they continued, they might be deterred from committing the murder, and the crime actually might not result in a killing. This supplemental argument suggests that the contentions of the two parties, which would seem on their face to be largely concerned with technical construction, were underlaid with considerations of the effect of the statutory provisions on future criminal conduct.

After more than a year of appeals and legal argument, Wang An-shih's views prevailed. A Yün's sentence was reduced by two degrees, and under the system of reduction applicable under the Sung code she presumably served a period of penal servitude. The victory cannot be regarded as one of jurisprudence, since it marked only one of the aspects of the consolidation by Wang An-shih of his position as the emperor's first minister. His opponents included in memorials to the emperor complaining about the administrative and political unreliability of Wang An-shih an attack on the position Wang had taken in the A Yün case, but their appeals were unavailing.

The distinguished Ch'ing Dynasty jurist, Shen Chia-pen, believed that from the viewpoint of statutory analysis Wang An-shih's position is untenable. Among the points Shen made were the following:

1. A killing results, except perhaps in the case of madmen, always from a certain reason. Intentional killing (that is, manslaughter), just like planned killing, is not conceivable without a certain causative reason. Planning and killing therefore cannot be separated into separate elements as Wang argued while at the same time conceding, as Wang did, that intentional killing is a unitary causeless crime.

2. Through his strained division of all crimes of killing into separate elements of cause and killing, Wang An-shih came into difficulty in the case of killing in an affray, which was punished more leniently than intentional killing. The statute provided no basis for Wang An-shih's attempt to resolve this difficulty by the assertion that in all cases in which the original penalties were more lenient than those for intentional killing, the original penalties remained applicable even in the event of confession.

One of the most remarkable features of Imperial Chinese criminal law is the persistence of the major provisions through the centuries. The statutory provisions relating to the effect of confessions, over which Wang An-shih and Ssu-ma Kuang struggled so mightily, remained substantially unchanged through the end of the last dynasty, the Ch'ing, in 1911. It is unlikely, however, that Wang An-shih's ingenuity in splitting up the elements of homicide provisions left much impact on the later centuries. An interesting decision declining to subdivide the elements of a crime was rendered in the case of Liang Ya-ju in 1818.

In that case the defendant dirtied the clothing of Liang Ts'ai-hsien with unclean water, for which (not too surprisingly) "he was upbraided by the latter." He retaliated with such foul language that Ts'ai-hsien "in a state of shame and rage, killed himself." The defendant, learning that he was wanted by the authorities under a charge of inducing suicide by foul language, turned himself in and confessed. It was argued in his behalf that use of abusive language was a causative crime separable from the suicide and that the confession entitled the defendant to remission of punishment for the abusive language. The Board of Punishments, however, held that the elements of abusive language and the resulting suicide were related so closely that the offense was a unitary crime not subject to subdivision.

It is beyond question that many of the points made against the arguments of Wang An-shih, from the point of view of technical statutory analysis, are difficult to answer. Wang appears to have strained to achieve a result that would moderate the rigors of the applicable system of penalties. His contemporaries, just as they would not concede that public spirit motivated his economic reforms, found in his defense of A Yün an irresponsible purpose to upset established legal tradition. A contemporary account states that when a courtier heard of the victory of Wang in A Yün's case, he held his forehead and said sarcastically: "The legal provisions that have been abused for several centuries have at last today received their correct interpretation."

Modern scholarship has restored substantial respect for Wang An-shih's economic programs while acknowledging that the results he sought were in many cases frustrated largely as a result of corruption and lack of cooperation in the ranks of the bureaucracy. It is likely that continuing scholarship will also give greater recognition of his efforts to modernize and humanize the legal system.

Wang held a view of human nature that was a mixture of realism and hope. He did not believe, as Mencius, that people are born to be good nor did he believe, as Hsun Tzu, that human nature is basically evil. He believed instead that we are born with capabilities for good or evil which are developed by experience. In view of our power to change the dominant traits of our character, Wang placed great value on repentance and regarded the return of a sinful person to virtue as the reclaiming of a potentiality born in him. He wrote: "If it is unreasonable to say that wealth once lost and later regained, is not the owner's rightful possession, can it be reasonable to say that virtue, which belongs by right to man's original nature, once lost, and later restored, is not the achievement of his original nature?"

Although it would be wrong to ignore the political setting of Wang An-shih's defense of A Yün, it would be equally shortsighted to deny that his attempt to avoid the harsh criminal penalty traditional legal interpretation would have required was consistent with his preference for reform over criminal punishment.

"The Sinister Behind the Ordinary": Emlyn Williams's *Night Must Fall*

The compelling title of *Night Must Fall* sounds like a literary quotation, but it is actually the result of a painstaking search by actor-playwright Emlyn Williams for the simplest way of expressing the idea that had inspired the play: "the sinister behind the ordinary." Although all the characters in *Night Must Fall* talk about murder, it is to the introspective Olivia Grayne that Williams assigns some of his own characteristic comments on the manner in which murder is perceived by the "ordinary" person. When Olivia learns that a murder has been committed in the neighborhood, she finds it hard to grasp the idea that "there's a man walking about somewhere, and talking, like us; and he woke up this morning, and looked at the weather." In her mind a comfortable workaday belief that murder is unreal alternates with a darker knowledge that it coexists intimately with her and threatens the disruption of her living pattern: "No, murder's a thing we read about in the papers; it isn't real life; it can't touch us . . . but it can. And it's here. All round us. In the forest . . . in this house. We're . . . living with it." And yet when murder ultimately intrudes into her life, Olivia's emotion is less that of horror than of surprise at its banality. "And that's murder," she says. "But it's so ordinary. . . ."

Emlyn Williams's ability to present both the terrifying and the depressing aspects of murder was formed by a close study of criminal cases and the masterworks of English crime writing. He had once thought of dramatizing the crimes described by Thomas De Quincey in his classic essay *On Murder Considered as One of the Fine Arts*. However, as an aspiring young actor, Williams had a good reason for putting the De Quincey project aside: he wanted to write a play of his very own, starring his "very own self." For the facial picture of his murderer he did not have to look far. He tells us: "I put the fag-end between my lips and looked in the mirror." The mirror did not lie to him, for Williams played the role of the murderer with great distinction in the original London production, which opened at the Duchess Theatre on May 31, 1935 with Dame May Whitty as Mrs. Bramson and Angela Baddeley as Olivia Grayne. These players also appeared in the New York run at the Ethel Barrymore Theatre, which began in October 1936.

Night Must Fall builds suspensefully to the murder of an elderly hypochondriac, Mrs. Bramson, by Dan, a hotel page boy whom she has taken into her isolated Essex bungalow as an attendant and flatterer. In order to provide a realistic quality to his drama, Williams drew on his memories of many English murder cases of the preceding fifteen years. Because of his immersion in crime history, we can believe what the play tells us about the murders it depicts; the actuality that was furnished by his sources was far worse. For details about the disposal of a corpse, Williams had cast his mind back to Patrick Mahon's murder of his mistress Emily Kaye in a Sussex bungalow (1924) and to Toni Mancini's clumsy concealment of the body of Violette Kaye (alias Joan Watson) in his Brighton lodging (1934). In fact, it was Patrick Mahon's crime that gave Williams the idea for what was to become one of the most celebrated (and certainly one of the most horrific) props in modern stage history—the hat box in which a previous victim's head is hidden.

In the personality and motivation of Williams's murderer we can see reflections of at least three cases in which a young man killed an elderly woman for gain. The earliest of the cases was that of Henry Jacoby, an eighteen-year-old pantry boy in a London hotel, who was executed in 1922 for battering to death a hotel guest, Lady Alice White, as she lay in her bed. The prosecution argued that Jacoby had gone to Lady White's room to steal but murdered her when she awakened. Jacoby excited considerable public sympathy because of his youth and possible insanity. He claimed that he had heard "whisperings" in the hotel basement earlier in the night, and that he entered Lady White's room because of murmurs he thought indicated the presence of "some other person who had no right to be there."

Certainly no sympathy need be wasted on John Donald Merrett, another of the models for Williams's murderer. Tried in Edinburgh in 1927 for the shooting of his mother, whose bank accounts he had been draining away by clever forgeries, the nineteen-year-old Merrett was freed by the ambiguous verdict permitted under Scottish law, "not

Henry Jacoby, a hotel pantry-boy whose murder of Lady White
was one of the sources of *Night Must Fall.*

proven." (This grudging verdict has been waggishly translated as "not
guilty, but don't do it again.") Merrett's criminal career, like the play it
inspired, was remarkable for its revivals. In February 1954, almost three
decades after his first escape from the law, the middle-aged Merrett
(now known as Ronald Chesney) was found, shot dead, in a wood near
Cologne, Germany, after a police hunt occasioned by his murder of his
wife and mother-in-law two weeks before.

Amid the numerous murderers Williams identifies as the originals of the villain of *Night Must Fall* he has generally given first place to Sidney Harry Fox, the Margate murderer. Williams had some indirect personal knowledge of Fox. A middle-aged acquaintance of the playwright had picked Fox up at a London bar in 1929 and about a year later had the unpleasant experience of opening his morning paper to find that Fox stood charged with having murdered his mother by setting fire to her hotel room. An accomplished forger, confidence man, and thief who liked to pose as a member of high society, Fox had served a number of prison terms. In March 1929 upon his release from prison he took his mother Rosaline on a curious odyssey from hotel to hotel, always moving without paying their bill. Finally, Fox had just about run out of potential victims except his mother. On October 21, he left his mother ensconced at the Metropole Hotel in Margate and went to London to arrange for the extensions of two insurance policies on her life for a suspiciously short period—until midnight of Wednesday, October 23. He then returned to Margate, where he accomplished the murder of his mother with precise timing worthy of a veteran quarterback working the two-minute drill. At 11:40 P.M. on Wednesday, twenty minutes before the insurance expired, Fox rushed downstairs into the lobby to report a fire in his mother's room. Her body was quickly brought out into the hallway but she could not be revived. At first Fox won sympathy as a grief-stricken son, but the tide soon turned against him. While the doctor was examining his mother's body, the hotel manager's wife consoled Fox by stroking his hair. When she prepared for bed that night, she was surprised to find that her hand smelled strongly of smoke and the next morning she reported her suspicions to the police. A close inspection of Mrs. Fox's room indicated that the fire had been started intentionally and her body was ordered exhumed. Famed forensic scientist Sir Bernard Spilsbury found evidence that Mrs. Fox had been strangled and the fire had been set to create an appearance of accident. Though other doctors contested Spilsbury's conclusions, Fox was convicted and hanged. The outcome had undoubtedly been influenced by Fox's emotionless demeanor in the witness box, and by his incredible statement that on discovering the fire, he closed the outer door of his mother's room so that "the smoke should not spread into the hotel." Fox's callous courtroom behavior is probably reflected in the Lord Chief Justice's speech, which serves as a brief prologue to *Night Must Fall*.

Williams obviously delighted in accumulating true-crime footnotes for his play. In his article for the October 1936 issue of the American theatre magazine *Stage*, written prior to the opening of *Night Must Fall* in New York, he claimed to have found inspiration for the play in a hearing of a murderer's appeal he had attended with the distinguished crime writer F. Tennyson Jesse. Sidney Fox did *not* appeal, and the hearing described by Williams in *Stage* bears some resemblance to the appeal in the Rattenbury-Stoner case which was heard in London in June 1935 after *Night Must Fall* had already opened there. For the Paris version of the play, Williams hit on the idea of changing the murderer into an ice-cream vendor, as was the case in the Le Touquet forest murder. (I regret that he missed the opportunity of choosing for the title of the adaptation *The Bad Humor Man*.)

All this raw material obviously required considerable reworking for the stage. Williams had started off with the murderer and his second victim as son and mother but rejected the plan on the ground that "absolute truth in the theatre can be too shocking." But as he worked at his final design of the relationship, he did not stray too far from his original intent, for the murderer cynically but effectively casts himself into an imitation of a filial role. Moreover, his victim's niece, Olivia Grayne, and her other visitors and attendants express feelings of extreme hostility towards her. "She'll be found murdered one of these days," Olivia's phlegmatic suitor Hubert Laurie correctly predicts, and Olivia cannot restrain herself from saying to Dan, "I could kill her." These angry words recreate much of the atmosphere of pervasive hatreds that is the hallmark of family murder cases. The hostility of the onlookers to the murder victims is made palatable in *Night Must Fall* by Williams's application of a theory held by many crime writers—that many victims have personal characteristics that attract murderers. Williams's friend F. Tennyson Jesse coined the term "murderee" to describe such victims and wrote that for every trunk murderer there is a victim who is "trunkable," a person who may be nice but is probably "rather foolish and wanton" as well. Of the victims in *Night Must Fall*, one suffers from twin manias (dipso and nympho), and the other is in such an advanced stage of bullying hypochondria that, as Dan observes, the only remedies left are artificial respiration and chocolates. Actually, the theory that victims attract murderers through the failings of their own personality is a consoling one since most of us consider ourselves free of defects, but, as the twentieth century has progressed, we have learned that victims, whether of individual or mass murder, can be distressingly random.

I think that we will remember Williams's murderer longer than his victims. The author's directions note that his personality varies considerably as the play proceeds. The first impression he makes is of totally disarming good humor and childlike unselfconsciousness, but, Williams warns us, "it would need a very close observer to suspect that there is something wrong somewhere—that this personality is completely assumed." The mystery about the murderer's name and origins, and his addiction to playacting, underscore the fact that he has a weak sense of his identity and lives largely in a world of his imagination. He is extravagantly vain and completely preoccupied with the impression he is making on others, to the point that he foregoes a chance of escape so that he can indulge in a tirade of self-praise for his murderous accomplishments. Yet he is capable of exerting a strong personal appeal, not only by his good looks and charm, but also through quick insight into the vulnerabilities of others. For a demanding and gullible old woman he can posture as a "son" and a flatterer. His relationship with Olivia is much more complex; though superficially he acts the role of a lady's man pursuing a woman of repressed passion, he also shows uncanny insight into the affinities between their personalities. Olivia and he are both lonely, rebellious, resentful of their subordinate stations, and deeply insecure. To her secret penchant for poetry he offers his flair for "speechifying" and he can even match his insomnia and nightmares with hers. The final irony of their interplay is that, though Olivia is afraid of violence, the murderer is even more intensely afraid of the hundreds of people watching behind each tree, the thousands of eyes, the "whole damn world" on his track.

The first evening notice of *Night Must Fall* in Edinburgh, where the play previewed before its London opening, appeared under the headline "Can a Woman Love a Murderer, Problem of New Play"; the reviewer reported that when the murderer kissed the heroine without being repulsed, some women in the audience said, "Absurd." Those women must never have read of the love letters commonly received by real-life mass murderers, and surely cannot have seen *Richard III*.

Lully and the Death of Cambert

Musicians have not been immune to the venom of professional rivalry. Tradition appears to attribute the most intense rivalries to operatic composers. In the case of one of the great competitive pairings, Gluck and Piccinni, neither man seems to have had any basis to reproach the other for acts of unfairness. The guilty parties were the factions of the Paris opera world which attempted unsuccessfully to pit the two men against each other in an operatic *mano a mano* by assigning them the same libretto based on Quinault's *Roland*. The legends of other rivalries are darker. In the accounts of the enmity of Salieri for Mozart and of the victory of Jean-Baptiste Lully over Robert Cambert, we read not only testimonies to professional antagonism but also hints or outright charges of assassination.

The Mozart-Salieri traditions have been summarized elsewhere. However, the story of how Lully came to be blamed for the death of Cambert in London in 1677 is relatively little known to the English-reading public. Moreover, little effort has been made by prior researchers (principally French) to determine whether the tradition that Cambert had died violently can be documented from English records. My two purposes here will be to summarize the anti-Lully traditions which have grown up around Cambert's death and to demonstrate, on the basis of a survey of English records, the difficulty of producing evidence that Cambert was murdered by anyone.

It is not an accident that the most extreme traditions of musical rivalry from the seventeenth and eighteenth centuries derive from the world of opera. Many factors fed the potentialities for conflict that are never wholly lacking when sensitive artists are struggling to find acceptance for their work. Due to the cultural centralism of monarchic society and the great expense of opera productions, the commissioning and subsidization of operas were primarily under control of the court. The success of opera composers was accordingly determined not only by talent but also by the political strength of their supporters. Courtiers electioneered for the opera composers under their patronage and their campaigns were marred by "dirty tricks."

The passions that were stirred by opera politics were further inflamed by nationalism. In the seventeenth and eighteenth centuries, Italian opera, and Italian operatic composers and troupes, were exported to the major European capitals, where they met with native resistance. To the extent that this led to adaptation of Italian style or development of newer national styles, such resistance was musically fruitful, but it also took its toll in personal animosities directed against the cultural invaders. The libels against Salieri were based in large measure on his Italian origin. Lully was not able, either by his writ of naturalization from Louis XIV or the changed spelling of his name, to convince the people of Paris that he had, "in spite of all temptation to belong to other nation," become a true Frenchman.

The story of the competition of Cambert and Lully for mastery of the French opera world might read like the race of the hare and the tortoise if we were to attribute more cunning to the tortoise than is granted by proverb. Cambert was off the mark thirteen years sooner, but rested for a decade, and when success was in sight, his more resourceful adversary overtook him.

Cambert's musical career in Paris was anchored by significant official posts. He served as organist of the Church of St. Honoré, and from 1662 or 1663, as Anne of Austria's Master of Music. Early in his career Cambert conceived the idea of creating a *comédie en musique* in the French language. Under Cambert's concept, musical continuity would be provided by the use of recitative on the Italian model, and the singers would move freely about the stage instead of striking wooden postures. Cambert's first effort in the new operatic genre, written to a libretto by the clumsy and conceited poet Pierre Perrin, was the so-called *Pastorale of Issy*, which was performed at a private country home at Issy near Paris in 1659. Unfortunately, Cambert was never inclined or able to push the borders of opera beyond pastoral scenes. A second opera, *Ariane et Bacchus*, was composed in 1659 under a commission from Mazarin, but its performance was called off after Mazarin's death.

Cambert did not turn to opera again until 1669. In this year he renewed his association with Perrin, who in June 1669 had obtained a royal *privilège* authorizing him to organize an *Académie de musique* for the production of opera. In March 1671 Cambert and Perrin presented their opera *Pomone* as the inaugural work of the *Académie*. *Pomone* was immensely successful and may have enjoyed more than seventy performances within an eight-month period.

It is speculated that the success of *Pomone* encouraged Lully to enter the opera world and make it his own, to the exclusion of Cambert and other possible rivals. However, he might have arrived at the same destination in any event, though his route was circuitous. The narrative of the spectacular rise of Lully from obscurity is well known. A son of an Italian miller, Lully was brought to Paris as a youth to serve Mademoiselle de Montpensier (la grande Mademoiselle) as an Italian tutor and attendant. Having displayed musical precocity while in her employ, he was astute enough to change sides during the Wars of the Fronde and to enter the service of the young Louis XIV. Enjoying Louis' admiration and affection, Lully began as dancer, ballet director, and orchestra conductor and became an important court composer, both of ballets and ceremonials and of incidental music to the comedies of another favorite of Louis XIV, Molière. About the same time as the premiere of *Pomone*, Lully's *Psyche* was produced. Although ballet and stage machinery remained dominant, critics are agreed that elements of opera were also present in the work.

Somehow, Lully became convinced that he should acquire the Perrin *privilège* and fashion a wider musical monopoly for himself. It is not clear whether the idea originated in Lully's own ambition, or in the encouragement of Colbert or Mme. de Montespan or Louis XIV himself. Lully always attributed the idea to the king, and it would certainly have been consistent with the king's belief that each important task of the nation, whether political or cultural, should be exclusively committed to trusted hands.

In any event, Lully's original acquisition of the Perrin *privilège* cannot be regarded as a wrong to Cambert. The theatre partnership that had been operating under the *privilège* had been torn by dissension, Perrin was languishing in debtors' prison, and Cambert's role in the venture had been reduced to that of a hired musician (hired, but, alas, not paid). Lully worked out a businesslike agreement with Perrin for the transfer of the *privilège* in consideration for Lully's discharge of Perrin's debts. Lully's transgressions against his musical colleagues, including Cambert, arose not from his agreement with Perrin but from his ruthlessness in obtaining and enforcing a new royal *privilège* of unparalleled scope. Under this new authority, and undeterred by litigation brought by his adversaries, Lully closed the theatre at which *Pomone* had triumphed, raided its opera troupe, drove all competing opera composers from the field, and even placed severe restrictions on musical accompaniment in the theatre of his old collaborator, Molière.

The musical career of Cambert in London has been traced, as well as the scanty records permit, by André Tessier and W. H. Grattan Flood in separate studies published in 1927 and 1928. Cambert arrived in London in either 1672 or 1673. He was possibly influenced to make this move by the fact that his student Louis Grabu was Master of the King's Music at the court of Charles II. In the fall of 1673, Cambert founded in London a so-called "Royal Academy of Music" in which he held the post of director. This institution was an essentially private opera theatre, although Cambert appears to have enjoyed for a time a measure of royal patronage, which may have included a loan of stage sets. The high-sounding name Cambert chose for the theatre was undoubtedly intended to reflect some of the authority of the Parisian operatic monopolies, and apparently served its purpose at least posthumously by misleading historians into attributing to Cambert an official position as royal director of music at Charles's court.

In the early spring of 1674 Cambert's Royal Academy presented his opera *Ariane*, which had been modified with the assistance of Grabu, at the new Royal Theatre in Bridge's Street (Drury Lane). This theatre had been built to replace an earlier theatre that had been destroyed by fire in 1672. It appears that *Ariane* was performed in the French language by a troupe of French musicians who had been assembled by the Academy. Cambert's destiny to remain obscure was mirrored by the libretto, published in London in 1674, which identifies Grabu as the sole composer. The libretto bears a prefatory letter to Charles II dedicating the work of the Academy to his service and signed, perhaps too optimistically, "your Academy of Music." It may be that other works of Cambert were performed in London in his early years there. It is possible that *Pomone* and *Les Peines et Plaisirs de l'Amour* were also produced in London, and a surviving libretto attributes to Cambert's pen a portion of a *Ballet et Musique pour le Divertissement du Roy de la Grande Bretagne* performed at the Court in 1674.

Unfortunately, Cambert's royal favor seems to have been short-lived. In August of 1674, his mainstay at the court, Grabu, was abruptly dismissed as Master of the King's Music and replaced by Nicholas Staggins, an Englishman. After 1674 Cambert is lost from sight until April 1677, when *le Mercure galant* reported his death with a resounding eulogy:

Jean-Baptiste Lully.

> Let us say that Music is unfortunate this year in every way, and that if some musicians have lost their lawsuits, others have lost their lives. M. Cambert, master of music of the late Queen Mother, has died in London, where his genius was greatly esteemed. He had received many benefits from the King of England and from the greatest noblemen at his Court, and all that they had seen of his work did not belie in the least what he had done in France. It is to him that we owe the establishment of the operas that we see today. . . .

This necrological article did not impute to Lully a role in Cambert's death. However, both in his historical assessment of Cambert's achievement and in a possibly ironic linking of Cambert's death to another man's suffering at the hands of Lully, the writer of the article appears to have intended to identify Cambert in death both as the superior of Lully and as his enemy. The assertion that France owed to Cambert the establishment of its operas obviously amounted to a rejection of the claims of Lully to that distinction. Not content with this critical judgment, the article delivered a personal blow against Lully by comparing Cambert's loss of life to another musician's loss of a lawsuit. This reference was clearly to Lully's judicial persecution of Henri Guichard, a business associate of Pierre Perrin who had held an interest in Perrin's theatre and royal opera franchise.

Lully, in order to counter Guichard's opposition to his opera monopoly, had initiated a criminal proceeding against Guichard for an alleged attempt to murder him by the administration of poisoned snuff. The poisoning plot, if it existed at all, was carried forward with all the clumsiness one associates with murder conspiracies in opera librettos. If there was any truth in the accusation, it is likely that the plot was, after feeble beginnings, largely an invention of Lully himself for the purpose of entrapping his adversary. The allusion in the *Mercure*'s Cambert necrology to Lully's legal victory was based on the fact that Guichard had been convicted of the attempted poisoning in September, 1676, but the comment was premature: Guichard appealed and was exonerated by the appellate court within a month after the appearance of the article. However, the association that had been made between Cambert's death and Lully's own charge of foul play against Guichard was to bear fruit in the creation of a murder legend.

Lully died in 1687. His death was marked both by praise and bitter invective. One of the most extravagant literary tributes was an account of Lully's reception into the Elysian Fields by the great departed spirits of music. Possibly in response to this piece or similar exercises in hyperbole, a poet and humorist, Antoine Bauderon de Sénecé, published in 1688 a satirical account of what *really* happened to Lully in the Elysian Fields. Sénecé's little book is in the form of a letter from the sixteenth-century court poet, Clément Marot, to the editor, circumstantially specifying as place and date of mailing, "Elysian Fields, April 20." In describing Lully's entry into the Temple of Persephone, Sénecé, like the Cambert necrologist, makes a reference to Lully's charges against Guichard, and he leaves no doubt as to his feeling with regard to their lack of substance: "Barely had he [Lully] taken a few steps when he was seen to change color and to show on his countenance more fear than he had ever had for the alleged poison of Guichard."

Persephone's Temple was the Elysian tribunal at which judgment was passed on the qualification of a new entrant to be granted immortality. Lully's advocate was the Italian musician Balthasar de Beaujoyeulx who, like Lully, had found favor at the French court. Beaujoyeulx appears to have been a rather maladroit spokesman, since he spiced his eulogy with Sénecé's own animus. When Anacreon opposed Lully's claims on the ground that Lully refused to recognize the primacy of the poet's contribution to opera, Beaujoyeulx rejoined that Lully was well aware of the important role of poetry: why else would he have headed his scores with laudatory verse epistles to Louis XIV?

At this point, Pierre Perrin's spirit stepped forward, and, still bitter over the loss of his opera rights to Lully, urged that, far from being entitled to immortality, Lully should be punished "as the thief that he was of the labors and reputations of others." Perrin's final charge that Lully had used his opera monopoly to "cut the throat of so many" is immediately taken up in a melodramatic intervention by the tortured ghost of Cambert:

> "Yes, yes, cut the throat!" a furious shade cried in a terrifying outburst, and, breaking through the crowd, was immediately recognized as that of poor Cambert, still entirely disfigured by the wounds that he had received when he was in England. "You see, Madame," he continued in the same tone, "to what end I was brought by the tyranny of Lully. The applause that I received from the public for the merit of my compositions aroused his indignation. He wanted to seize the fields that I had prepared, and reduced me to the cruel necessity of going to seek my bread and glory in a foreign court, where envy found a way of finishing, by depriving me of life, the crime that it had begun by exiling me from my homeland. But regardless of whose hand struck the blows that took my life, I shall never impute them to anyone but Lully, whom I regard as my real murderer, and against whom I demand that you give justice. And it is not for myself alone, Madame, that I implore your equity; it is in the name of all those who distinguished themselves in their times by some rare ability in music, whom he never ceased to persecute by all sorts of means."

This passage can be read, like the *Mercure* necrology, as falling far short of a murder accusation against Lully. The "crime" of which Lully is most clearly accused is that of having driven Cambert into exile by unfair competition, and in Sénecé's view, this crime also entails moral responsibility for Cambert's death in exile, regardless of the identity of the actual assailant. But the author's reference to "envy" as a common element in the crimes of exile and murder, either intentionally or by design, created an ambiguity. Did Sénecé mean to imply that minions of Lully pursued Cambert to London to complete his destruction, or that Cambert fell victim of envy from musical circles in London as he had done in Paris?

The various strands of Sénecé's multiple innuendos were taken up by later historians and his fictional account of a lacerated ghost became the surrogate of a corpus delicti. The historians do not acknowledge their debt to Sénecé and it is understandably embarrassing to footnote an assertion of murder by reference to a satirist. But the mark of *The Letter of Clément Marot* is everywhere to be seen in the commentaries on Cambert's death from the eighteenth century onwards.

In 1705, Le Cerf de La Viéville, a great admirer of Lully, developed the anti-English possibilities of Sénecé's charges, perhaps in the belief that he would thereby deflect blame from Lully. While Sénecé had left ambiguous the source of the "envy" which had destroyed Cambert, Le Cerf pointed his finger directly at Cambert's English competitors:

> Cambert seeing himself of no use in Paris after the establishment of Lully, moved to London, where his *Pomone* [*sic*], which he presented there, attracted to him considerable evidences of friendship and favor from the King of England and the greatest nobles of the Court. But the envy that is inseparable from merit cut short his days. The English do not find it good for a foreigner to intrude into their entertainment and instruction. The poor fellow died there a little earlier than he would have died elsewhere.

The Brothers Parfaict in their *Histoire de l'Académie royale de musique* paraphrased the above passage from Le Cerf de La Viéville, and also referred to a rival tradition that Cambert had been murdered by a valet. This second tradition (a parallel to the familiar mystery-novel formula that "the butler did it") leaves open the question as to whether the servant was acting for himself or for an undisclosed principal, and some whispered that the murderer was engaged by Lully. In addition to all the mysteries this theory summons up as to the details of hiring and escape of the murderer, the valet legend makes us wonder how Cambert, obscure as he was in 1677, could have afforded a manservant.

A less sensational residue of the Sénecé satire is a tradition that Cambert died of heartbreak in his London exile. This version leaves those who adopt it free to blame Lully or not, as they choose, depending on their views of Lully's musical merits and of the fairness of the steps he took to win and enforce his operatic monopoly.

Although none of the modern authorities attributes Cambert's death to Lully, a surprising number assume that Cambert was murdered. No evidence is cited in support of this assumption and it is hard to escape the conclusion that it is based solely on Sénecé's book. The writers accepting Sénecé may well have asked: would Sénecé have dared to describe the bleeding Cambert while his survivors still lived if Cambert had died peacefully or in his sleep? After all, it is one thing to speculate about a poisoning when a man has died suddenly (as in Mozart's case) and quite another to make vivid reference to knife wounds when Cambert's family presumably had seen his body and could tell the public whether he had been stabbed.

In view of the fact that Cambert's allegedly violent end came in London, it is odd that the tradition of his murder appears to be an exclusively French product. My researches in London libraries and record offices have not uncovered any evidence either that Cambert was murdered or that there were any rumors to such effect current in London at the time of his death.

Although exhaustive searches might prove more successful, I have not found any English record of his death or burial. At the time of his death, burial records were maintained by individual parishes, of which there were more than 100 in London and its environs. None of the published or unbound parish burial registers for London or Middlesex County that I have reviewed contain any record of Cambert's death or burial, nor do the will indexes list any will in his name. In fact, the only surviving official English record I have discovered with relation to the Cambert family in or after 1677 is a note in the State Domestic Papers of the grant of a passport for France to Cambert's daughter, Marianne, on December 1, 1678.

Cambert's death came too early in journalistic history for us to expect to find a story on his death (however lurid it might have been) in the London newspapers. The most important journal, the semi-official *London Gazette*, devoted most of its space to news of the wars of Louis XIV. Unfortunately, however, it contains no news of Cambert's death. Accounts of murders were not considered appropriate daily fare for the *Gazette*'s readers. However, if Cambert had indeed been murdered by a valet who had committed the additional capital offense of stealing plate or linens from his master's household, notice of the theft would have been permitted to appear among the *Gazette's* frequent advertisements for runaway servants and stolen household goods.

The absence of newspaper coverage of crime in the late seventeenth century was compensated for by a welter of pamphlets devoted to murders and executions. These pamphlets are indexed by Donald Goddard Wing in his bibliography of seventeenth-century publications. The name of Cambert does not appear in the index. There is no reference to criminal proceedings arising out of Cambert's death in the selective edition of the records of the Middlesex Sessions, and a search made at my request of the surviving indictments in the Court of King's Bench during the Hilary Term of 1677 (January through March, 1677) was also unproductive.

The principal English diarists also make no reference to Cambert's death. Robert Hooke, friend of Sir Christopher Wren and Samuel Pepys, was in London in early 1677 and made daily entries in his diary during the period. He was an aficionado of crime, if we can judge by an entry in 1677 referring to "H. Killigrews man stabbd next the Kings bedchamber" and by his speculation in a 1679 diary page on the motive for the murder of Sir Edmundbury Godfrey. However, Hooke's diary does not mention Cambert's death.

Therefore, in the scales against Bauderon de Sénecé's vivid description of Cambert's wounds we place the English silence. Silence is capable of conspiratorial interpretation, particularly if we accept the strand of French tradition that implies that Cambert was disposed of by English rivals. However, it is a strain on credulity to suppose that conspirators, however highly placed, could have imposed a total censorship not only on official records but also on gossip, one of the most highly-developed arts in London. If we are to reconcile the possibility of Cambert's murder with the apparent disregard of his death in London, we must hypothesize that by 1677 Cambert had fallen into obscurity; that his murderer was unknown and went unpunished; and that there was no inquiry into the circumstances of his death. In view of the difficulties presented to research of the records of this period, these possibilities cannot be excluded. However, unless evidence of murder should some day be discovered in England, it will remain difficult to accept not only the libels against Lully in the matter of Cambert's death, but also the more widely accepted hypothesis that he died a violent death by someone's hand.

A century after Cambert's death, Sir John Hawkins set down what can still serve as the official English view of the Cambert affair. According to Hawkins's account, Cambert "died, with grief, as it is said, in 1677." The source of his grief was the rejection of his work by the English public. Hawkins found no fault with the public's judgment. Ironically, Hawkins paired the antagonists Lully and Cambert as co-workers in a style that could not fall pleasingly on English ears:

> Perhaps one reason of the dislike of the English to Cambert's Pomone, was that the opera was a kind of entertainment to which they had not been accustomed. Another might be that the levity of the French musical drama is

but ill suited to the taste of such as have a relish for harmony. The operas of Lully consist of recitatives, short airs, chiefly gavots, minuets, and courants, set to words; and chorusses in counterpoint, with entrées, and splendid dances, and a great variety of scenery; and, in short, were such entertainment as none but a Frenchman could sit to hear, and it was never pretended that those of Cambert were at all better.

Hawkins's chauvinistic rejection of French taste was matched by his outrage at the tradition, stemming from Le Cerf de La Viéville, that Cambert had been done away with by envious English musicians. Referring to a republication of Le Cerf's innuendo in Bourdelot's music history originally published in 1715, Hawkins comments wryly on the hypothesis that English musicians envied Cambert: "A modest reflexion in the mouth of a man whose country has produced fewer good musicians than any in Europe."

It is appropriate that this tale of the musical animosities of Italy, France, and England should end on a note of nationalism.

Fouquet's Trial in the Letters of Madame de Sévigné

When Mme. de Sévigné, whose brilliant correspondence is one of the great literary treasures of the reign of Louis XIV, wrote to Nicolas Fouquet, the secretary of finance, she could hardly have thought that her letters would one day fall into the hands of the police. Her words were not compromising, for the cautious widow had long kept the amorous Fouquet at bay. As early as 1655 she had commented humorously, in true *précieuse* spirit, on the reserve she was maintaining in their relationship: "In my dealings with him, I still show the same wariness and timidity, so that the progress he would like to make is appreciably delayed. I think that in the end he will get tired of always beginning again at the same point and in vain." Six years later, at the time of Fouquet's arrest, correspondence from Mme. de Sévigné was found in a letter-casket during a search of the fallen minister's house at Saint-Mandé. Unfortunately, the letters of the virtuous lady were discovered in doubtful company—interspersed with notes from mistresses declaring their ardor and reports from female spies, gossips and go-betweens who did Fouquet's bidding in the wings of court life. In a letter that nestled close to those of Mme. de Sévigné in the famous casket, one of Fouquet's mistresses, Mlle. de Menneville, a lady of honor to the Queen Mother, remarked pointedly: "You cannot doubt my friendship without offending me to the point of fury, after the tokens which I have given you of it." And many of the casket letters came from Fouquet's devoted intriguer, Mme. Laloy, who reported the arrangements she had made to spy on his great rival Jean-Baptiste Colbert: "A *valet de chambre* of the duc de Bournonville, who desires to leave his master, has told me that he is

MARIE DE RAB...UTIN CHANTAL
MARQUISE DE SÉVIGNÉ
Née à Paris en 1626   Morte à Grignan en 1696

Mme. de Sévigné.

entering the service of M. Colbert, and has promised to tell me everything that happens there."

The discovery of her letters to Fouquet in such unwelcome circumstances could not fail to flurry the customary serenity of Mme. de

Sévigné. She responded to her worry in a predictable manner—by dashing off a letter, in this case to her Jansenist friend, Simon Arnauld de Pomponne. She asked him what he had to say about all the things that had been found in the casket:

> Would you ever have believed that my poor letters, full as they were of M. de La Trousse's marriage and his family affairs, would be put in such a mysterious place? I confess that whatever credit, in the opinion of those who do me justice, I may derive from never having had any dealings with him, I am none the less deeply concerned when I find that I am obliged to justify myself—and perhaps entirely in vain—before hundreds of people who will never realize the truth of what I say.

Although this letter strongly registers her alarm at Fouquet's imprudent handling of her correspondence, any irritation that she might understandably have felt towards him was quickly submerged in her concern for his fate. For Fouquet faced grave charges that might cost him his life—dishonesty in the administration of his country's finances, and treasonous plans for a civil war in the event of his arrest. Suspicions of Fouquet's financial irregularities had been fostered for years by Colbert, who coveted his office. Colbert had heralded his campaign in 1659, during the premiership of Mazarin, by writing the cardinal a long *mémoire* detailing abuses in the system of finances and proposing establishment of a special court to dispense the punishments necessary to assure reform. In the course of the *mémoire* Colbert cited public knowledge that Fouquet "has made great establishments not only for himself, for his brothers, for all his relatives and friends, and for all agents who have approached him, but also for all persons of quality in the realm whom he has wanted to win over."

Although Colbert had not yet attacked him to his face, Fouquet took a number of impulsive actions that made it clear he regarded himself as the principal target of his rival's complaints. After he obtained a copy of Colbert's *mémoire* from the postmaster, who was in his pay, Fouquet had the audacity to complain to Mazarin of Colbert's opposition. Not content with this direct approach, which left Mazarin flabbergasted, he turned next to the Queen Mother, Anne of Austria, making a bid for her support through a pretended "confession" of formal irregularities which he attributed to the critical conditions faced by the treasury during the Wars of the Fronde.

But it was even before the launching of Colbert's attack that Fouquet took an action that showed most melodramatically an awareness of his jeopardy: he began to draft and revise a plan to incite a civil war in the event of his downfall and to detach Brittany in his cause. Justifying his mad project by his need to protect himself against the "distrustful and jealous" Mazarin, who was easily induced to have every bad impression of those who held a considerable post in State affairs, Fouquet meticulously listed the members of the nobility who should be asked to come to his aid should an emergency arise, and gave instructions on fortifications of towns and the mustering of troops. In 1658, after his acquisition of Belle-Île off the Breton coast, he made additions to his draft, in which he broached some sensational new schemes, including the possible kidnapping of some of his principal enemies among the Councillors of State.

After the death of Mazarin, Colbert lost no time in communicating his charges against Fouquet to the young King Louis XIV. It was at this point that Fouquet failed to observe one of the clearest rubrics laid down by criminal history: If you are an embezzler, don't invite the boss for a weekend in the country. In 1661 the king accepted Fouquet's invitation to attend a fête that the minister was preparing at his chateau at Vaux. Fouquet's natural extravagance allied itself with a great love of the arts, and Vaux was the masterpiece of his life. The chateau was set among elegant formal gardens by Le Nôtre, and three villages had been razed in sacrifice to the grandeur of the prospect. The ceilings of the chateau were painted by Le Brun; and the dinner service beggared the Louvre. The cultural high-point of the fête was an open-air performance of *Les Facheux* by Fouquet's friend Molière. The king moved from one surprise to another, but his host saved the climax for his royal guest's evening departure. As the court party took the road the dome of the chateau was suddenly illuminated and shot off a multitude of fireworks that enflamed the entire horizon. Whether the insolent display of wealth at Vaux played a decisive role in winning the king over to Colbert's plans we cannot know. It was only a few weeks after the fête that Fouquet was arrested at Nantes, with a high degree of secrecy and military precaution that can only have been inspired by fear that news of his fall would touch off a coup d'état. When his home at Saint-Mandé was searched for incriminating evidence, the *commissaires* of the king not only found the innocent letters of Mme. de Sévigné, but behind a mirror they came upon Fouquet's draft of civil war plans, which he thought he had burned.

For three years the investigation and trial of Fouquet dragged on amid clear signs that the king and his partisans would let no obstacles of legal tradition stand in the way of a death penalty. After Fouquet's personal papers were seized certain of them were removed with the approval of the king so that the accused could not use them in preparing his defense. Moreover, the minister, whose commission of office explicitly made him answerable only to his sovereign, was not placed on trial before a regularly constituted panel of the Parlement but instead required to face a special tribunal packed with his enemies and the king's creatures, including Henri Pussort, the uncle of Colbert. The charges against him proliferated at a dizzying rate. It must have become apparent early to the prosecution that the treason charge would not be sustained. After all, was not the civil war plan a treason of the mind, the product of an imagination sickened by the disorders of the Fronde and fears of Mazarin's unreliability, and had not any wisp of potentiality that Fouquet's schemes ever had blown away when the cardinal died? But, as the treason charges faded the accusations of financial misdeeds multiplied. It was claimed that Fouquet had made the king imaginary loans and received interest that was not due him; that he had commingled royal funds with his own and used them for his private extravagances; that he had extracted pensions from tax collectors as the price for closing his eyes to their irregularities; that he had, without authority, reissued at par outdated treasury obligations which he had purchased at a low price.

The final weeks of Fouquet's trial, in November and December, 1664, are documented in a remarkable series of letters from Mme. de Sévigné to M. de Pomponne, who had been involved in Fouquet's disgrace and had been banished from Paris in 1662. So far as we know, Mme. de Sévigné did not attend any of the trial sessions, which were held at the Arsenal in Paris, but from the circumstantiality of her commentary it is apparent that she had reliable information from friends at court. What aspects of the trial interested her? She can be pardoned for not passing along to M. de Pomponne the details of the complex evidence and argument bearing on the charges of financial maladministration; her references to the topics of cross-examination are in any event sufficiently precise for us to identify the phases of the prosecution's charges to which they relate. But her mind and heart were elsewhere. In the foreground of her account was the figure of her "poor friend" Fouquet, and she delighted in recording his verbal triumphs over his questioners. She also took special pains to treat M. de Pomponne to sharply etched portraits of the heroes and villains of the trial; to convincing reconstructions of courtroom eloquence; and to dramatic renderings of unexpected turns in the trial proceedings. Of legal technicalities we read little in her letters with the exception of her accurate description of Fouquet's challenges to the court's jurisdiction. The omission of legal particulars is quite understandable; Mme. de Sévigné saw clearly that the trial was guided less by law than by politics, and her letters exposed the shifting political currents of the case as they moved through the Arsenal courtroom or the halls of the Louvre itself. All these various strands of the case—of personality, courtroom drama, and political maneuver—are drawn together into a taut narrative by the use of the concise style for which Mme. de Sévigné is justly famous. Indeed, as she began her account, she warned herself not to be led by her strong emotions into loquacity: "I feel that I am seized with a desire to talk, and I must not give in to it: the narrative style must be concise."

It is the lonely figure of Fouquet that holds center stage when Mme. de Sévigné's surviving narrative of the trial begins with the second appearance of the defendant in the witness-chair (*sellette*) on November 17. At once she emphasizes the outstanding traits of his courtroom behavior: courage, self-possession, articulateness, and a wary avoidance of the traps laid by his adversaries. As Fouquet maintained his challenge to the authority of the special tribunal, the presiding judge, Chancellor Pierre Séguier, an old personal enemy, interrupted him to ask whether he charged the king with an abuse of power. Mme. de Sévigné reported Fouquet's moving response: " 'It is you who say it, sir, not I. The thought never entered my mind and I am amazed that in my present state you should wish to get me into trouble with the King.' " For Mme. de Sévigné, Fouquet's responses were always "convincing" and "excellent," laying bare the weakness of the charges against him. However, supremely witty herself, she reserved her greatest admiration for his wit. She found particular enjoyment in retelling his triumph in a verbal duel with the chancellor over the treason charge. In fact, so anxious was she to transmit an accurate rendering of Fouquet's words on this occasion that several days after giving a brief contemporaneous account she furnished de Pomponne an expanded version. It appears that Chancellor Séguier, during the Fronde, had conspired with the Prince de Condé to arrange for the introduction of a Spanish army into France in opposition to the Royal forces. When Séguier asked Fouquet to concede that his drafted civil war project constituted treason, the defendant responded, according to Mme. de Sévigné:

> "I admit that it is sheer madness and extravagance, but not treason. I beg these gentlemen," said he, turning towards the judges, "to allow me to explain what treason is. . . . it is treason when a man, occupying one of the supreme offices of State and enjoying the confidence of the monarch, suddenly takes over the leadership of his enemies' council; when he commits his whole family to the same cause; when he has the gates of towns of which he is Governor opened to hostile armies and closed in the face of his real master; when he betrays all State secrets to his own party; that, sirs, is what is called treason."

Mme. de Sévigné added that Séguier, stung by the allusion to his political past, "did not know where to put himself, and all the judges wanted to laugh."

In the background of Mme. de Sévigné's courtroom narrative move, on the one side, the secondary figures of the contending judges, the partisans of the king, and Colbert attempting to rush the trial to a conclusion, and on the other the courageous recorder, Mme. de Sévigné's relative Olivier d'Ormesson, who in her account is virtually the only spokesman for judicial fairness. Mme. de Sévigné neatly captured the quality of the justice being meted out to Fouquet when she quoted the impetuous exclamation of Judge Pussort at the end of Fouquet's testimony: "Thank God! there can be no complaints that we did not hear him out." Mme. de Sévigné was prompt to render her own ironic judgment: "What do you think of those fine words? Do they not suit an excellent judge?"

In counterpoint to the proceedings at the Arsenal, Mme. de Sévigné kept M. de Pomponne up-to-date on the more meaningful struggle being waged at the Louvre over Fouquet's life. On Wednesday, November 19, the court did not sit because the queen fell dangerously ill. Fouquet's mother gave the queen a plaster "which cured her of her convulsions; strictly speaking they were vapours." Fouquet's wife and mother lost no time in attempting to turn their cure to the advantage of the defendant, for the very day of the queen's recovery they sought out the king, but Mme. de Sévigné reported that he "ignored these poor women when they threw themselves at his feet." As it turned out, the best the plaster could accomplish was to produce smiles on the faces of the Fouquet partisans in the courtroom. A few days later, the chancellor, ever on the attack, remarked: "Here is a matter on which the accused will be unable to answer." Recorder d'Ormesson, alluding to defensive evidence that would meet the chancellor's charge, remarked knowingly, "Ah! sir, here is the plaster that can cure it."

Mme. de Sévigné understood that no cure was likely for Fouquet's plight unless it came from the king, and from him she expected little justice or mercy. It is astounding how frankly Mme. de Sévigné committed to paper her unflattering impressions of the king. Perhaps she trusted to the secrecy of her mail deliveries, although at least in some cases there is evidence that she used prearranged initials or nicknames in referring to public personages. More likely she had a high order of bravery and self-confidence that the despotism of the new king's regime had not quenched. Not only did she show him unfeelingly spurning the petitions of Fouquet's wife and mother, but she also reported his interference with the trial; she wrote that the court clerk had circulated a document written by the king warning that he would be displeased should any of the judges base favorable verdicts on the removal of certain of Fouquet's papers on the king's orders. But to Mme. de

Sévigné the king's greatest shortcoming was his unawareness that his courtiers would never give him their honest opinion. It is a fine effect of her narrative genius that this failure of the king's intelligence is made apparent in a small incident that is in itself unrelated to the Fouquet drama. One day while the case was proceeding the king handed the Marshal de Gramont a copy of a madrigal and asked him whether he had ever seen one so tasteless and whether he did not think the author a conceited fop. The marshall hastened to agree with his sovereign's literary judgment, and then the king with a laugh said that he had written the poem himself. When the flustered marshal asked for a second look at the poem, blaming his critique on too hasty a reading, the king only continued to laugh at his discomfiture. Mme. de Sévigné reported that everyone thought this "the cruelest little thing that could be done to an old courtier." Then she added her own more perceptive comment on the anecdote: "For my part, as I always like to meditate on things, I wish the King would do so about this and learn from it how far he is likely to be from ever knowing the truth."

Although her reports of the trial were second-hand, Mme. de Sévigné could not resist the suggestion made by some ladies that she go with them to a house overlooking the Arsenal in order that she could catch a glimpse of her "poor friend" on his way back to prison at the end of the day's proceedings. She was masked, and saw Fouquet coming a fair way off, escorted by d'Artagnan and fifty of his musketeers. As they drew near, the ever courtly d'Artagnan touched his prisoner and let him know that the ladies were there. Mme. de Sévigné then describes their sentimental encounter: "So he bowed to us and smiled with the expression you know. I do not think he recognized me; but I confess I was strangely moved when I saw him go in at that little door."

Mme. de Sévigné's masked greeting to Fouquet was far from marking the limit of her personal participation in his case. Passages in the letters reveal that she was directly made aware of a secret attempt to influence the verdict in the defendant's favor and that she made at least one intervention on her own. Séguier, the hostile presiding judge, was given to religious ecstasies between court sessions. Indeed, Mme. de Sévigné confesses that she would love to have invented the *bon mot* that was making the rounds in Paris: "Pierrot (Pierre Séguier) [is] transformed into Tartuffe." The mother superior of the convent of Sainte-Marie de Sainte-Antoine told Mme. de Sévigné the details of four visits Séguier had paid her during the last months of the trial. On one occasion while the chancellor protested of his longing for salvation, the mother superior "spoke to him cleverly about M. Fouquet's case." The mother superior asked Mme. de Sévigné (vainly as it turned out) "not to make this little story public knowledge." It is left to our surmise whether Mme. de Sévigné encouraged the mother superior to continue her efforts at Séguier's conversion. In any event, there is no doubt that Mme. de Sévigné attempted to work her considerable persuasive powers on her relative Olivier d'Ormesson, who was one of two recorders at the trial. The recorders, lawyers charged with preparing the official reports of the evidence, were also voting members of the court panel. Mme. de Sévigné seems to have pressed the conscientious d'Ormesson too far for, in her letter of December 5 to de Pomponne, she confesses: "M. d'Ormesson has asked me not to see him again until the verdict is reached; he is in the conclave and does not wish to have any further dealings with those outside it." But Mme. de Sévigné flattered herself that her words were not lost on him: "He affects great reserve; he speaks not a word, but listens, and, in saying good-bye to him, I had the pleasure of telling him plainly what I think."

The dramatic highlight of Mme. de Sévigné's account of Fouquet's trial is her report of the summations of the evidence by the recorders and the casting of the votes by the judges, an agonizingly slow process that was the subject of five letters to M. de Pomponne between December 9 and 20, 1664. Her relative M. d'Ormesson was the first of the two recorders to have the floor and "he spoke with extraordinary directness, intelligence and ability." But the signs seemed ominous to Mme. de Sévigné. One of the judges, Colbert's uncle Pussort, interrupted him several times, and at one point when he seemed to speak in Fouquet's favor, interjected: "We shall speak after you, sir, we shall speak after you." D'Ormesson bore Pussort's provocation in silence, but Mme. de Sévigné reported (perhaps on the basis of a conversation with d'Ormesson she had wheedled despite his ban on further contacts) that had he been interrupted once more he would have answered: "Sir, I am here to judge, not to denounce." To Mme. de Sévigné's mind d'Ormesson had seen the light "only when the case was past curing."

On Monday, December 15, d'Ormesson and the other recorder, Sainte-Hélène, were to render their verdicts and then the judges were to begin to vote. But on Saturday Mme. de Sévigné reported that the enemies of Fouquet on the court had decided on a last-minute tactical move. D'Ormesson would give his judgment today, so that Sainte-Hélène could begin fresh on Monday and start the ball rolling toward a death sentence. M. d'Ormesson cast his Saturday vote for a lenient punishment—banishment for life and forfeiture of the accused's property to the king. In so doing, according to his admiring relative, the lawyer had "set a crown upon his reputation."

But by the following Wednesday Mme. de Sévigné was "languishing in anxiety." She reported that on Monday and Tuesday Sainte-Hélène, d'Ormesson's "very unworthy colleague," had "spoken indifferently and feebly, reading his speech, and neither adding anything new or giving a new twist to the affair." Without giving any reason, he voted for beheading but then, to hedge his bets, the trimmer added that "no doubt the King would show mercy and that he alone could do so." Mme. de Sévigné added that Wednesday morning Pussort delivered a four-hour tirade against Fouquet that was so violent that "several of the judges were horrified, and people think his fury will do our poor friend more good than harm." Yet surprisingly, after asserting that "rope and gibbets were [the] only adequate punishment," Pussort opted for Sainte-Hélène's suggestion of royal clemency because of the high offices Fouquet had held.

While she nervously awaited the remaining votes, Mme. de Sévigné regaled M. de Pomponne with the rumors and distractions that helped Fouquet's admirers through the last difficult days of the trial. A comet had been appearing for four days; characteristically, Mme. de Sévigné had not seen the new wonder herself but heard of it from "M. de Foix, who saw it in company with three or four scientists." Turning to stories being circulated regarding personages of the trial, she told of Fouquet's archenemy Berrier, who "has gone mad, quite literally" and, despite blood-letting, raved about gallows and was even choosing trees for the purpose. She mentioned a criminal reportedly offered an acquittal in exchange for damning testimony against Fouquet, and told of the heroism of one of Fouquet's judges named Masnau, who dragged himself to court half dead with "nephritic colic" and during a brief court recess "passed two stones so large that indeed it might have been a miracle, if men were worthy of God's working them."

On Friday, December 19, Mme. de Sévigné wrote to M. de Pomponne of her "great hopes," and embarked on a review of the judges' votes with the skill of a practiced political analyst. When she was on political ground we can feel sure that she was not merely quoting opinions of others, as she so often did, but was thinking for herself. She had already made this plain in her letter of December 9, in which she disassociated herself from the premature optimism of Fouquet's family and her friend, the *précieuse* novelist Mlle. de Scudéry:

> I have seen them; I have been amazed by them. They seem never to have known or read what happened in times past. What astonishes me more still is that Sappho [Mlle. de Scudéry] is just the same—she whose intelligence and shrewdness are unlimited. When I think over it again, I delude myself and am convinced—or at least I want to be—that they know more about it than I do. On the other hand, when I reason it out with others less biased, whose judgment is excellent, I find the scales so finely balanced that it will be a miracle if the case turns out as we wish it to. Cases are always lost by one vote, and that one vote is everything.

When she wrote her letter of December 19, there was a stronger basis for predicting the outcome of the trial. She reported that on Thursday four judges had voted for death before Judge Roquesante "after speaking admirably for more than an hour, . . . adopted M. D'Ormesson's opinion." Six votes for death, two for exile. But then this morning, it seemed to Mme. de Sévigné that "we were sailing with the wind, for two or three who were doubtful made up their minds" and all at once there were five more votes for exile, including one from the heroic victor over his kidney stones. As the day drew to a close, it was the turn of a hardliner named Poncet to speak, but he put off his task until Saturday, for he was afraid that the remaining speakers were favorable to Fouquet and, according to the shrewd Mme. de Sévigné, "did not wish to lose public favour by voting for the death penalty unnecessarily." Summarizing the situation at the close of the day's session, Mme. de Sévigné concluded optimistically, "We have seven; they have six. Among [the remainder] there are more on our side than we need." She was right in her prediction, and on Saturday gave M. de Pomponne a happy bulletin: "Praise God, sir, and thank Him: our poor friend is saved. Thirteen voted like M d'Ormesson, and nine like Sainte-Hélène. I am beside myself with happiness."

But the ending of the story was not to be so bright for Fouquet and his friends. The next day Mme. de Sévigné informed M. de Pomponne that the king had "commuted" the sentence from exile to life imprisonment and that Fouquet was to be taken to Pignerol Prison on Monday. With her customary bravery she bitterly commented, "Against all the rules, he is not allowed to see his wife." As Fouquet took the road for prison, her thoughts remained with him. She wrote to de Pomponne that D'Artagnan was his only consolation on the journey and she cheered herself with hearsay that "the man who is to guard him at Pignerol is very decent." Throughout the years, long after his trial had turned from news into history, she continued to write of Fouquet and the vain efforts of his family and friends to alleviate his lot. Finally in April, 1680 she wrote to her daughter, Mme. de Grignan, the sad news of his death: "Here is still more sadness, my dear daughter. M. Fouquet is dead; I am touched by it; I have never seen so many friends lost."

It was Mme. de Sévigné's sympathy for her old friend and admirer that infused her reports of Fouquet's ordeal with a humanity that professional journalism can only rarely equal. However, her sympathy for the victims of criminal justice had distinct limits. Perhaps we cannot classify as a "victim" the infamous poisoner the Marquise de Brinvilliers, who was beheaded at Paris in July, 1676. Mme. de Sévigné's letter to Mme. de Grignan written on the day of the execution reveals a mixture of emotions. She described her reaction to the sight of the condemned woman:

> At six o'clock she was taken, wearing only her chemise and the rope round her neck, to Notre-Dame, to make her public confession. Then, in a low mob-cap and chemise, she was put back into the same tumbril (in which I saw her) and thrown face upwards on some straw, with a theologian beside her and the executioner on the other side; to tell the truth, I trembled at the sight. Those who saw the execution say she mounted the scaffold very courageously.

This expression of pity for a murderess overwhelmed by the machinery of public retribution, and of admiration for her fortitude, comes as a surprise after the levity of the letter's opening: "Well, it is all over, Brinvilliers is in the air: after the execution her poor little body was thrown into a very large fire, and her ashes scattered to the winds; so we shall inhale her, and by absorbing the little vital spirits we shall become subject to some poisoning humour, which shall surprise us all."

When Mme. de Sévigné wrote to her daughter of the ruthless suppression of the peasant rebellion in Lower Brittany, her customary tone of cheerfulness prevailed. She reported with equanimity how twenty-five or thirty men were seized "at random" to be executed and how the authorities, sated with breaking people on the wheel and quartering their bodies, had turned to plain hanging. Her main concern during these times of troubles was that her enjoyment of nature remain undisturbed: "The rebels of Rennes fled long ago; and so the good will suffer in place of the wicked; but I find all this satisfactory, provided the four thousand soldiers who are at Rennes under M. de Forbin and M. de Vins do not prevent me from taking walks in my woods, which are of marvelous height and beauty."

Sainte-Beuve, one of the greatest nineteenth-century admirers of Mme. de Sévigné's genius, was disappointed that "on this occasion Mme. de Sévigné's heart unfortunately failed to rise above the prejudices of her time." In her favor, however, he notes that she occasionally intervened in behalf of galley prisoners, of whom the most interesting was a young man from Provence who was devoted to Fouquet and received a five-year sentence for delivering him a letter from Mme. Fouquet. In this instance, as in her letters on the trial of Fouquet, Mme. de Sévigné's sympathy was aroused not by a sense of abstract justice, but by her keen interest in everything that concerned her close friend. This is all that one should expect from the heart of this delightful woman, for Mme. de Sévigné's world was a world of friends.

The Janitor's Story: An Ethical Dilemma in the Harvard Murder Case

If we are to believe the Indiana humorist George Ade, patriots can be competitive even about their countrymen's crimes. Ade tells us of the shipboard traveler from Emporia, Kansas who tartly responds to an Englishman's criticism of violence in the United States by observing that "there were fewer Murders in England because good Opportunities were being overlooked." Of course, quantity has never been synonymous with quality, and the well-behaved British may be forgiven for the belief that their murders, relatively few though they may be, include inimitable cases—from the Brides in the Bath to Ten Rillington Place. But for the most intriguing of these cases the American patriot would have a worthy rival to put forward—the Harvard Murder Case of 1849.

The Harvard Murder Case is rightly named because most of the cast of characters were Harvard men: the defendant, the victim, the trial judges, counsel on both sides, and twenty-five of the witnesses (including Dr. Oliver Wendell Holmes). The defendant, John White Webster, was a professor of chemistry at Harvard University and at the Harvard Medical College in Boston. The victim, Dr. George Parkman, was a benefactor of the medical college who drew his wealth from real estate investment and private moneylending. His generosity as a philanthropist was matched (and probably facilitated) by his relentlessness as a creditor; one of his slow-paying debtors was Webster, who had exhausted what little patience Parkman had by fraudulently selling off a mineral collection he had mortgaged as collateral for his borrowing.

On Friday, November 23, 1849, Parkman disappeared. He had stopped off that day at a shop near the medical college to purchase "a quantity of lettuce, a rare plant at that season," for an invalid daughter to whom he was much attached, and was last seen alive entering the medical college between one-thirty and two in the afternoon. When Parkman, a man of regular habits, did not return home, his family and friends became alarmed. The next day the police were notified of his disappearance, and a wide search was undertaken. Handbills were issued offering a reward of $3,000.

On Sunday, Webster informed Dr. Parkman's brother, Francis, that the missing man had called on him by appointment at the medical college at half past one on Friday and that Webster had settled his debt by paying him $483. The search continued during the course of the following week. Webster's rooms at the medical college were inspected, the river was dredged, and a thorough search was made of the yards, outbuildings, and houses in the western part of Boston, where Dr. Parkman had large real estate investments (and perhaps other defaulting debtors). The police inquiries extended as far as sixty miles throughout adjacent towns. While the police flailed about without success, an unexpected ally was at work. The janitor of the medical college, Ephraim Littlefield, whose living quarters were adjacent to Webster's laboratory on the upper basement story of the medical college building, suspected that Parkman's body must be hidden somewhere on the premises and concluded that the only place that had not been inspected was the vault under Webster's privy. On November 29 (the Thursday after the disappearance) he set to work to pierce the privy vault and on the next day completed a breach of the wall. Inside the vault, near the opening he had made, Littlefield found certain remains of a human body—a pelvis, the right thigh and the left leg from knee to ankle—and certain towels marked with Webster's initials and similar to those used by the professor in his laboratory.

On Friday evening and Saturday morning, the police also found in an assay furnace (a furnace used to test metals) in Webster's laboratory, fused with slag and cinders, a great number of fragments of human bones and certain blocks of false teeth. Later on Saturday, they also discovered in a remote corner of the laboratory, in a place they had previously noticed but not examined, a tea-chest that contained, imbedded in a quantity of tanning material and covered with minerals, the thorax of a human body, a left thigh, and Webster's hunting knife. Around the thigh bone was tied a piece of twine similar to that found in one of Webster's drawers. The various remains were examined and found to be parts of a single body that resembled the body of Parkman. Dr. Keep, Parkman's dentist, identified the false teeth found in the furnace as part of a set that he had prepared for the missing man.

Webster was arrested and charged with the murder of Parkman.

Prof. John W. Webster.

From his cell, he accused Littlefield either of committing the murder or conspiring to fix the guilt on him. Webster was represented at his trial by two well-known members of the Massachusetts Bar, Edward D. Sohier, who had been primarily a civil lawyer, and Pliny Merrick, a judge of the Court of Common Pleas. Merrick had greater criminal experience than Sohier, having served as district attorney, but Sohier took the role of lead counsel, because he had represented Webster in certain matters in the past. After an eleven-day trial, the jury deliberated for a little less than three hours and returned a verdict of guilty; Webster was sentenced to be hanged. An appeal was made in his behalf to the governor for commutation of the sentence, and in the course of that appeal, in which Webster had initially asserted his innocence, a confession of the murder was ultimately filed with the Committee on Pardons of the Massachu-

Dr. George Parkman.

setts Executive Council. That confession was promptly labelled a "hoax" by much of the press, because it contained some puzzling factual assertions and also was viewed as a last-ditch effort by Webster to save his life. In any event, clemency was denied, and Webster was hanged on August 30, 1850.

Obviously, the key to the case against Webster had been Littlefield's discovery of Parkman's remains, and therefore the centerpiece of the trial was "the janitor's story." Although the presiding judge, Chief Justice Shaw, suggested in his charge to the jury that "the facts and circumstances" that the janitor discovered "constitute the substance of the evidence," the judge cannot have failed to notice from Littlefield's testimony that his search for the body was oddly motivated and spasmodically performed.

Littlefield testified that he had been employed as janitor of the medical college for seven years and had known the defendant during that period; he had been acquainted with Parkman for twenty years. He was present at an interview between Webster and Parkman on the Monday prior to the disappearance. He heard Parkman ask, "Dr. Webster, are you ready for me tonight?" Webster answered, "No, I am not ready tonight, Doctor." Parkman accused Webster of selling or remortgaging collateral, and warned him as he left that "something must be accomplished tomorrow." Littlefield also said that, on the same Monday and before Parkman called, Webster had asked him a number of questions about access to the vault under the dissecting room of the medical college. The following day Webster asked Littlefield to carry a note to Parkman.

On Friday morning, November 23, as Littlefield set his broom behind the door to Webster's back room off the chemistry lecture room, he noticed a sledgehammer that was usually kept in the laboratory below. The sledgehammer thereafter permanently disappeared, and Littlefield's recollection of its unusual whereabouts on the fatal Friday appeared to contain a gratuitous suggestion of its possible use as the murder weapon. Other signs of hostility to the defendant are scattered through the janitor's testimony, but in view of the accusations Webster had made against him, the witness's irritation is understandable.

The janitor further stated that on the afternoon of Friday, November 23, towards two o'clock, he saw Parkman coming toward the college, "walking very fast" (a not inappropriate gait for a persistent creditor). Later, when he went downstairs to Webster's laboratory-stairs door, which led out into the janitor's cellar, Littlefield found that door and another door to the laboratory bolted on the inside. He thought that he heard Webster walking inside the laboratory and water running. About half past five, as he was coming out of his kitchen, he heard someone coming down the back stairs that led into the janitor's cellar; it was Professor Webster, holding a lighted candle.

On Saturday morning, Littlefield unlocked the door of Webster's lecture room and tried to get into his adjacent back room, but found it locked. Presently, Webster arrived, a small bundle under his arm, and unlocked the door to the back room. He asked the janitor to make him up a fire in the stove.

Littlefield testified that on Sunday evening he had a conversation with Webster that aroused great misgivings in him. Webster asked him whether he had seen Parkman during the latter part of the preceding week, and the janitor told him that he had seen him coming toward the college about half past one on Friday. The professor then volunteered that this was the very time that he had paid Parkman $483 and some odd cents. The janitor was struck with Webster's unusual demeanor: "Usually, when Dr. Webster talks with me, he holds his head up and looks me in the face. At this time, he held his head down, and appeared to be confused, and a good deal agitated. I never saw him so, before; that is, look as he did: My attention was attracted to it. I saw his face, and I thought that he looked pale." On Monday, the janitor tried twice to get into Webster's room to make up his fires but found the doors bolted. On the same day Littlefield was in Webster's laboratory briefly on three occasions while visitors were calling in connection with the Parkman disappearance. The following day he was present during a police inspection of Webster's rooms; it seemed to him that when one of the police officers, Mr. Clapp, inquired about the privy, the professor "withdrew the attention of the officers from that place."

On Wednesday morning Littlefield saw Webster arrive at the college early and soon heard him moving things around in his laboratory. The janitor went to the laboratory door, tried unsuccessfully to look through the keyhole, and began to cut a hole in the door but gave up because he thought Webster had heard him. Later that day, as he was passing by, he found that the walls near Webster's laboratory were unusually hot. He thought that the fire must be coming from the assay furnace, where he had never known a fire to be, and was afraid that the building would take fire. He climbed the wall to the double window of the laboratory, found it unfastened, and went in. The first place he inspected was the assay furnace, in which he found only a small fire. He then examined two water hogsheads and found that two-thirds of the water was gone from one and that all the water had been drawn from the other. He also noticed that two-thirds of the pitch-pine kindlings in the laboratory were gone. As he went upstairs, his eye was caught by some spots on the stairs he had never seen before. Putting his finger to them, he found that they tasted like acid.

Thursday was Thanksgiving. In the afternoon, about three o'clock, Littlefield set about digging a hole through the wall of the vault under Professor Webster's privy. He testified in explanation of his action:

> I wanted to get under there to see if anything was there, and to satisfy myself and the public; because, whenever I went out of the College, some would say, "Dr. Parkman is in the Medical College, and will be found there, if ever found anywhere." I never could go out of the building without hearing such remarks. All other parts of the building had been searched, and, if nothing should be found in the privy, I could convince the public, that Dr. Parkman had not met with foul play in the College.

Using a hatchet and a chisel, he worked about an hour and a half but found he could not make much progress with these tools and gave up the job for the night. He went out that night and stayed up till four o'clock the next morning at a ball given by a division of the Sons of Temperance. About noon on Friday he had a conversation with Dr. Henry Bigelow of Harvard. He asked Bigelow whether he knew if there was any suspicion of Webster and Bigelow told him there was. Littlefield informed Bigelow that he had commenced digging through the wall and understood him to encourage him to continue with the work. He testified that he received similar exhortations from Prof. John B. S. Jackson. Armed with this moral support from the Harvard faculty, he asked a foundry worker, Leonard Fuller, to lend him a crowbar, hammer, and chisel. He went back to work and made rapid progress. When he broke through the last of the five courses of brick in the privy vault, he made his grisly discovery.

This testimony by Littlefield was a focal point of a withering attack made in the press and within the ranks of the legal profession on the conduct of the Webster trial. The criticism of the trial spared no one; Chief Justice Shaw, the prosecution, and the defense counsel all were subjected to abuse. In fact, the conviction of Webster led to a kind of regional warfare between the bars of New York City and Boston, with several New York lawyers leaping into print anonymously to savage the reputation of New England justice, and their Massachusetts colleagues rising against them in stout defense. One of the published diatribes against the Webster trial that won wide notoriety was a pamphlet entitled *A Review of the Webster Case, by a Member of the New York Bar* (1850). It is now known that the author was A. Oakey Hall, a colorful Harvard Law School graduate whom Tammany Hall was to elect mayor of New York in 1868. By a stroke of luck that often awaits the compulsive bookbuyer, I recently happened upon a scrapbook of Hall's memorabilia of the Webster trial containing his manually annotated copy of a trial report, a group of pamphlets (including his own *Review of the Webster Case*), law journal articles, and newspaper clippings. These materials provide a unique insight into the roots of Hall's criticism of the trial.

A principal target of Hall's attack was the "silence and timidity of cross-examination evinced by the counsel for the defense," each of whom, to his mind, perhaps "thought more of playing the polished gentleman than discharging the duty of the enthusiastic advocate; and kept ever in mind that decorum and courtesy were more important than the acquittal of their client." Hall was particularly sharp in his criticism of deficiencies in the cross-examination of Littlefield. He complained that the defense had not adequately probed the issue of the janitor's access to the scene of the crime. Why did they not press Littlefield about the circumstance that the dissecting-room was found unbolted the morning after Parkman's disappearance when it was bolted the night before? And if Littlefield could gain entry into Webster's laboratory on the famous hot Wednesday, could he not have done so on other occasions as well? Hall also argued that Littlefield's "whole tenor of mind" should have been "almost minute by minute from Friday to Friday brought into confessional." Hall's questions pressed on each other: Why had the janitor neglected to investigate the privy earlier? how did he come to hit upon the exact spot in the privy vault where the body would be found? would he not have found it easier to fit a key to the privy room, unnail the seat and lower a lantern than knock down the wall of the vault?

However, Hall's ultimate criticism was addressed to the failure to mount an all-out attack on Littlefield's credibility: "Why was not his life raked over from beginning to end; his ways of life investigated that his credibility might be securely known? Were the counsel fearful of a libel suit; or of an assault and battery; or a loss of popularity?"

It is not a simple matter to determine the extent to which Hall's denunciation of defense counsel's handling of Littlefield is justified. Hall probably did not attend the trial and appears to have based his judgments on his reading of an unofficial report of the trial by Dr. James W. Stone, which is bound into his scrapbook. Stone's account does not report questions put by counsel, and generally testimony is summarized rather than reproduced verbatim. However, a fair-minded study of even this inadequate record of the Littlefield cross-examination does not fully bear out Hall's charges. The defense's questioning of the janitor, which was handled mostly by Sohier, occupied virtually an entire day of the eleven-day trial. Chief Justice Shaw, in his charge to the jury, observed that Littlefield had been "much sifted by cross-examination."

Many of the questions Hall would have liked to see pressed seem to have been put by Sohier to the janitor. He dwelt on the apparent inconsistencies in Littlefield's narrative: that he had begun to suspect Webster on the Sunday after Parkman's disappearance; that on the evening of Parkman's disappearance, *even before he entertained such suspicion*, he had returned from a party and tried the door of Webster's laboratory; but that *after he became suspicious of the professor*, he had taken no affirmative steps to investigate until he started to chisel away at the privy vault on the following Thursday. Between Sunday and Thursday, Sohier emphasized, Littlefield had calmly accepted a gift of a Thanksgiving turkey from Webster even though he felt (as he implied in his testimony on direct examination) that this unusual show of generosity was intended to silence him. Moreover, in this same period, he had foregone opportunities to look around Webster's rooms during four visits there in the course of the week after the disappearance, despite the fact that on two of those occasions he was in the company of police officers and at least once thought Webster was trying to distract their attention. On the Wednesday when Littlefield entered the laboratory through a window to determine the source of the unusual heat, he did so only because he "thought the building was on fire." He noticed that the assay furnace was pretty hot, but (despite his suspicions) did not uncover the furnace because Dr. Webster had told him "never to touch articles, except placed upon a particular table." In addition to highlighting the witness's strange reluctance to investigate the premises whose barred doors had previously aroused his apprehensions, Sohier also asked whether Littlefield could not have obtained access to the privy room; and tested the odd coincidence that Littlefield breached the privy vault at the precise spot where the body lay.

But the cross-examination, taken as a whole, still seems unsatisfactory. At least in the summary of the testimony given in the two principal reports of the trial, Sohier does not seem to have probed Littlefield's state of mind and motivation but to have focused instead on the externals of his behavior, thereby permitting the witness to restate and reinforce the chronological narrative he had given on direct examination. The principal weakness was the failure to make a straightforward attack on Littlefield's credibility.

Littlefield's role in the events at the medical college was, of course, the heart of the problem for the defense. It was certain, as Attorney General Clifford conceded in his closing argument, "that, these remains being there, it must have been known to Littlefield or Webster." If the defense were to maintain that the body's presence was unknown to the defendant, they must attribute its deposit (if not the murder itself) to the janitor. But in the cross-examination only two faint jabs were made at the janitor's integrity. Early in his questioning, Sohier (probably attempting to establish a good reason for Webster having bolted his doors) asked Littlefield whether the professor had not caught him in his room at night playing cards. Littlefield made a lame attempt to evade the inquiry. "I decline answering that question; but I will say that I have not played any cards, in his rooms, this winter." The only other direct attack on the witness's character was made by co-counsel Merrick, who established at the end of the cross-examination that Littlefield had seen reward advertisements a few days prior to beginning his assault on the privy wall. However, it has been recently revealed by Judge Robert Sullivan, in his *The Disappearance of Dr. Parkman* (1971) that defense counsel rejected a more dramatic avenue of attack suggested by Webster in his voluminous trial notes addressed to Sohier. Webster asserted that Littlefield had for years been moonlighting as a "resurrectionist" (grave-robber) and had been supplying dead bodies to the Medical College. The professor theorized that Littlefield had bought Parkman's body in a sack (à la Rigoletto) and attempted to obliterate its identity after he discovered to his horror who it was. Perhaps Sohier and Merrick thought that this suggestion smacked more of melodrama than of evidence. In any event, they let the janitor leave the stand with his story essentially unshaken and without any strong indication as to why he would have murdered Parkman, deposited his body, or attempted to implicate Webster falsely in his death.

Merrick later attempted to plug this gap in the defense—by a lengthy attack on Littlefield in his closing argument. When the bluntness and the biting satire of the argument are compared with the apparent restraint of the cross-examination of Littlefield, it is tempting to speculate as to whether there may not have been a disagreement between Sohier and Merrick on the approach to this key prosecution witness. The possibility of a divergence of views is enhanced by the fact that it was Merrick who intervened towards the end of Sohier's cross-examination to confront Littlefield with the reward handbills and to suggest that they might have motivated his tardy attack on the privy vault. In Oakey Hall's copy of the trial report there are many handwritten marks and angry marginal comments on the Sohier cross-examination, but he made no annotations on the portions of Merrick's closing argument dealing with the janitor's story. Hall's charges of timidity are certainly not borne out by Merrick's onslaught against Littlefield, for Merrick stopped only slightly short of imputing the crime to the janitor:

> I regret Gentlemen, that my duty compels me to allude to the testimony of [Mr. Littlefield]. I regret that I am obliged to do so, because I am confident whatever is said about this has a tendency to point a suspicion toward him as

the perpetrator of this crime. Now, Gentlemen of the Jury, you must not misunderstand me. I will not take upon myself the fearful responsibility, in defending one man, to charge another with the same crime. Far be it from me to say that I will charge Ephraim Littlefield with this crime! Far be it, whatever may be the tendency of my comments, if the effect should be to fix it upon him—far be it from my intention to connect him with this crime! But, Gentlemen of the Jury, it is my duty to examine, and it is your duty to weigh, the testimony of this witness; and if there be anything which tends to affect the testimony of that witness, you must give it weight, whatever the consequences may be.

In addition to making this strong suggestion of Littlefield's guilt, Merrick also attempted to cast a raking light on Littlefield's obscure and conflicting attitudes towards Webster. He noted that, although Littlefield claimed that his suspicions were first aroused by his conversation with Webster on the Sunday after the disappearance, "you will find that his vigilance anticipated his suspicions, while they were followed by an unaccountable apathy and indifference." In discussing Littlefield's search of the privy vault, Merrick followed the lines of Sohier's cross-examination by noting how odd it was that Littlefield had not first made any effort to gain access to the privy room itself and how it was even stranger that the remains were found exactly in front of the breach he had made but a few feet from a perpendicular line dropped from the hole in the privy seat. He cast doubt on the prosecution's theory that the remains had been dropped from above: "Could they possibly have been placed there, in that particular spot, by any efforts through the hole in the privy?" But his most effective weapon in treating Littlefield's discovery of the remains was the irony with which he recalled Littlefield's inappropriate moods in the course of his grim search. On the first night of his labors the janitor broke off his work "to join in the amusements of the festival of the season; and, after actually dancing eighteen out of the twenty cotillons that occupied the night, returned to sleep quietly in his bed, in an apartment beneath which, he professes to have believed, were lying the bones of a murdered human being. . . ." On the following Friday morning, Merrick noted, Littlefield did not rise early to resume his work but chatted pleasantly with Dr. Webster who came into his room at nine o'clock while the janitor was still at breakfast. Merrick pointed out that, when Littlefield decided to obtain from Mr. Fuller more effective tools to finish the job, he said in jest that he wanted a crowbar to dig a hole in the wall to let in a waterpipe. Finally, Merrick suggested that Littlefield appeared to take special pains to dismiss all possible witnesses from the scene just before he completed his breach of the privy wall. The defense counsel raised dark suggestions about the significance of this conduct:

Did not Littlefield too well foreknow the information which he should soon have to communicate? Why else did he rid himself of the presence of all spectators? Why else would he have it that no human eye but his own should look into the vault, until he had first seen these remains there in safe deposit? Were not all things yet ready there for the inspection of others? These are fearful questions, of pregnant suggestion, of momentous import. I leave the answer to your own reflections.

I am left with the impression that Merrick's closing argument was sufficiently effective in its treatment of the janitor that Hall was unjust in passing over it in silence. However, a closing argument can do little to shake the credibility of an opposition witness who has not been successfully discredited on cross-examination. The question then remains why Sohier and Merrick did not make a stronger effort, while Littlefield was on the stand, to raise a substantial question in the jury's mind as to the witness's involvement in the crime or at least in the deposit of the body. By one of the strange quirks of legal history, it is possible that the answer to that riddle is to be found in the influence of another murder case that was tried a decade before in England, the famous Courvoisier case.

A Swiss valet, Francois Bernard Courvoisier, was charged in 1840 with murdering his master Lord William Russell in his bed in the fashionable Park Lane district of London. On the first day of the trial Courvoisier's counsel, Charles Phillips, sharply cross-examined a housemaid, Sarah Mancer, who had testified against her fellow-servant, Courvoisier. The next morning, prior to the resumption of the trial, Phillips had one of the most chastening experiences a criminal lawyer can have in the midst of a trial: Courvoisier confessed to him that he had committed the murder but in the same breath insisted that Phillips continue the defense. Phillips had a temporary failure of nerve and informed Baron Parke, one of the judges sitting in the case, of his client's confession and requested his advice. Parke was understandably annoyed with Phillips for breaching his client's confidence and prejudicing the judge's position but according to Phillips, told him that he was bound to continue the defense "and to use all fair arguments arising on the evidence."

On the third day Phillips rose to deliver his closing argument to the jury. The precise words he used on this occasion have been the subject of dispute to this day. It was charged by some, after the news of Courvoisier's confession became public, that Phillips had improperly expressed a belief in his client's innocence. But perhaps a more serious charge was that, despite his knowledge of his client's guilt, Phillips had reinforced his cross-examination of Sarah Mancer by casting a suspicion on her in the closing argument. The latter complaint was to some extent just although, in his closing speech, Phillips purported to disown his accusations even as he made them:

> I must beg that you will not suppose that I am, in the least degree, seeking to cast the crime upon either of the female servants of the deceased nobleman. It is not at all necessary to my case to do so. I wish not to asperse them. God forbid that any breath of mine should send, tainted into the world, persons perhaps depending for their subsistence upon their character. It is not my duty, nor my interest, nor my policy, to do so.

By chance the controversy over Phillips's conduct, which raged fiercely immediately after the trial, was rekindled in 1849 when Phillips published a belated justification of his actions. A whole range of ancient questions of professional ethics were faced anew in their most intractable form: Is it appropriate for a trial lawyer to express to a jury his belief in the merits of his client's cause? To what extent should a client's confession, or his counsel's knowledge of or belief in his guilt, restrict the scope of cross-examination or argument? How and where does defense counsel strike a balance between his duty to his client and his obligation not to cause wilful harm to witnesses or third parties?

The revived debate over the ethical issues of the Courvoisier case raised strong echoes in America, and Phillips's courtroom conduct and his subsequent disgrace were very much on the minds of the lawyers in the Webster case and of their critics. It is a reasonable hypothesis that the reluctance of Sohier and Merrick to attack Littlefield more zealously in cross-examination and to brand him in the witness box as grave-robber or murderer was influenced by a desire to avoid Phillips's pitfall. In fact, the controversy over Phillips's professional ethics was explicitly referred to by Attorney General Clifford in his closing argument: he alluded to "the great case of Courvoisier, for the murder of his master, Lord William Russell—that case which has made all Europe ring with strictures upon the conduct of the Counsel, whether just or unjust." Lawyers who deplored the performance of Webster's defense counsel cited the example of Phillips's aggressiveness amid extreme difficulties as a standard by which Sohier and Merrick must be found wanting. Hall's approval of Phillips's tactics is evidenced by his inclusion in his scrapbook of an article favorable to Phillips. But voices from the Massachusetts bar were heard on the other side of the question. Hall also placed in his scrapbook an article on the Webster case from a Massachusetts journal, *Monthly Law Reporter*, which, after referring to the renewed uproar over Phillips in the English press, commented:

> *Had Dr. Webster's counsel adopted the tactics of the English barrister, they might have saved their client*; nor do we believe that the world would have regarded them with less favor on that account. So wanton and unreasonable

is that fickle despot, public opinion! For the honor of our bar, we are glad that they did no such thing, and all the lampooners of New York and Philadelphia cannot harm them.

Significantly, Hall underlined only the words that are italicized, the words suggesting a lost opportunity to save Webster from the gallows.

There is something to be said for Hall's selective reading of this passage. The ethical problem faced by Webster's counsel was far different from the dilemma that confronted Charles Phillips when he delivered his final argument for Courvoisier. In weighing their duty to provide a vigorous defense of Webster against their responsibility not to inflict unnecessary harm on a possibly innocent prosecution witness, Sohier and Merrick did not have their consciences burdened with a client's confession. On the contrary, Webster had himself publicly and privately suggested Littlefield's responsibility for the crime. Moreover, the Webster murder case, unlike the Courvoisier case and perhaps most other criminal trials where guilt has been imputed by the defense to third parties, involved a crime whose physical setting made it reasonably certain that either the defendant or a specific third party (Littlefield) was responsible for the victim's murder or the deposit of his remains. Under these circumstances, the failure of Sohier and Merrick to make an all-out attack on Littlefield in cross-examination could well have been interpreted by the jury as a show of embarrassment with their defense. No evidence of guilt can be more devastating in the eyes of a jury than the uneasiness of defense counsel with their client's cause. In this respect, Sohier and Merrick, while doubtless undeserving of the full measure of Hall's abuse, may have failed to serve Webster adequately.

The witnesses who faced the cross-examination of Charles Phillips and Webster's lawyers were heard of again after the trials in which they had figured passed into history. Sarah Mancer paid a terrible price for her innocent involvement in the Courvoisier case. The *Examiner* of London reported of her: "The cloud was heavy over her, and it passed so slowly that her life never more escaped from it. She died in a madhouse, driven mad by the sufferings and terrors, . . . the persecutions . . . the harassing interrogations to which she was subjected preceding the providential discovery of the guilt of Courvoisier. . . ." But Littlefield was clearly made of sterner stuff. A press clipping included in Hall's scrapbook discloses that when an exhibition of waxwork figures of Parkman and Webster opened at Clinton Hall in New York City, "together with a perfect Model of the Medical College, Boston, in which the lamentable tragedy occurred," the celebrated janitor appeared as hired lecturer "to explain to the audience the particulars of the whole affair."

The New York newspaper commentary was scathing. But one report spared Littlefield so that points could be scored against the arch-enemy Boston. Littlefield, readers were told, was "not quite so shameless a fellow as we deemed him to be." After reading the comments of the Sunday press on his announced exhibition, he "had the grace to pack up his disgusting 'traps' and make himself scarce as quickly as possible." The newspaper gave him credit for a sense of shame and wished him better profit from his regular profession at the Harvard Medical College. With a salvo of local pride that echoed the line of defense Webster had wished his counsel to take, the writer concluded, "There is a greater demand for dissecting subjects in the Massachusetts medical colleges than for disgusting subjects in New York."

The Trial of Jane's Aunt

Jane Austen's maternal uncle, James Leigh Perrot, possessed two of the status symbols of the respectable Englishman, as listed by Jane in her unfinished last novel *Sanditon*: "symptoms of gout and a winter at Bath." Uncle James had a touching (but unrewarded) faith in the therapeutic powers of the waters of Bath, and he and Aunt Jane Leigh Perrot spent almost as much time at that famous resort town and spa as at their home in Berkshire called Scarlets. In the winter of 1799–1800 Bath was particularly unkind to Uncle James's ailment, because, instead of conversing with his well-born friends at the Pump Room or the Assembly Rooms or promenading on the Royal Crescent, he spent the season with his wife at the rude home of the warden of Ilchester Gaol. For Aunt Jane had been arrested in Bath in August 1799 on the inelegant charge of filching a card of white lace from the William Smith millinery shop.

In May and June 1799, Jane Austen and her mother had also visited Bath in the company of Jane's brother Edward and his wife. It was feared that Edward was following in his uncle's painful footsteps and was teetering on the verge of gout. Jane's letters from Bath to her sister Cassandra report on Edward's condition (she had no cause for worry since he lived until eighty-two), but for the most part they are given over to shopping notes, which serve as an ironic prelude to Aunt Jane's impending troubles.

On June 2 Jane reported that she "saw some gauzes in a shop in Bath Street yesterday at only 4d. a yard, but they were not so good or so pretty

Mrs. Leigh Perrot, aunt of Jane Austen.

as mine." She also compared the merits and prices of flowers and fruits as millinery ornaments and mentioned Aunt Jane's expert recommendation of a cheap shop: "Flowers are very much worn, and fruit is still more the thing. . . . A plum or greengage would cost three shillings; cherries and grapes about five, I believe, but this is at some of the dearest shops. My aunt has told me of a very cheap one, near Walcot Church, to which I shall go in quest of something for you." Jane concludes with a sketch of the fiercely competitive social conditions which sent the young Bath tourists in desperate search of embellishments: "I have never seen an old woman at the pump-room."

In Bath Street, at the corner of Stall Street, was a "haberdasher and milliner's shop," which bore over its door the name "William Smith" but which had been kept for two years by Miss Elizabeth Gregory. The shop had previously been owned by William Smith and his wife, Miss Gregory's sister. Mr. Smith had apparently fallen into financial difficulty and conveyed the shop to William Gye and Lacon Lamb, as trustees for his creditors. Gye and Lamb gave up the shop to Miss Gregory, who had already been a shop employee for three years. It is tempting to speculate as to whether William Smith's was the Bath Street shop to which Jane Austen referred in her letter of June 2, since it was at this shop that Aunt Jane stumbled into the clumsy arms of eighteenth-century shoplifting law.

On Thursday, August 8, Mrs. Leigh Perrot came to the Smith millinery shop between one and two o'clock in the afternoon. She asked Miss Gregory to let her look at some black lace that she had first seen the day before. She decided to buy the lace, which cost one pound nineteen shillings, and Miss Gregory asked her clerk Charles Filby to measure and wrap the lace. Aunt Jane paid for the purchase with a five-pound banknote and was given her package and change.

About a half hour later, the Leigh Perrots were passing the shop on the other side of the street when Miss Gregory crossed the street and addressed Mrs. Leigh Perrot: "Pray, ma'am, have not you a card of white lace as well as black?" Mrs. Leigh Perrot answered: "No, I have not a bit of white lace about me." Asked to "see" in her pocket, Aunt Jane gave a paper parcel to Miss Gregory, saying, "If I have, your young man must have put it up in mistake." Miss Gregory examined the parcel and found it contained not only the purchased black lace but also a card of white lace bearing her shop's private inventory marking. Aunt Jane insisted that the clerk had given her the white lace by mistake, but Miss Gregory replied: " 'Tis no such thing, 'tis no such thing, you stole it, you are guilty."

Miss Gregory took the white lace, leaving Aunt Jane with the black lace and the package. Within half an hour, she went with the clerk Filby to the Bath Town Hall to present a charge against Mrs. Leigh Perrot. The mayor was away, and they were told to come back the next day. Miss Gregory and Filby returned daily but were not successful in having their charges received until the following Wednesday, since the magistrates had their hands full making arrangements for the passage of a detachment of boisterous soldiers out of the town.

On Wednesday Miss Gregory and Filby finally obtained a hearing before the magistrates. A prima facie case of shoplifting was found to have been made out, and Aunt Jane was committed to Ilchester Gaol to await trial at the next county assizes to be held in the spring at Taunton. The offense on which Aunt Jane was to be tried was far from trivial. Shoplifting of an item valued at five shillings or more was a capital crime, and the white lace was put down in the indictment at twenty shillings. For capital punishment the price was right. Although the penalty would likely have been commuted to transportation to Botany Bay in Australia, subjection to the rigors of the penal colony could be equivalent to a death sentence for convicts whose constitutions were not hardy.

Aunt Jane's social position had not exempted her from commitment pending trial, but it did win her the privilege of lodging in the house of the warden, Mr. Scadding, rather than in the prison itself. She was joined by Uncle James, who bore bravely a new onslaught of gout as well as a quality of accommodations far below the most modest Michelin rating. Aunt Jane wrote of the indignities suffered by her fastidious husband: "Cleanliness has ever been his greatest delight, and yet he sees the greasy toast laid by the dirty children on his knees, and feels the small Beer trickle down his Sleeves on its way across the table unmoved." Aunt Jane declined the kind offer of her "sister Austen" to send her daughters Jane and Cassandra to stay with them. Aunt Jane had stated that she could not procure the girls accommodations in the warden's house with her, and that she could not let those "Elegant young Women" be inmates in a prison or be subject to the inconveniences she and her husband were obliged to put up with.

Indeed, the Leigh Perrots were themselves looking for a change of scene. In September, they went to London to seek an order from a judge of the King's Bench releasing Aunt Jane on bail. However, the request was turned down and Aunt Jane was remanded to prison. She wrote in disgust that "others must determine" whether the judge's refusal to grant bail was due to "inexperience or profound Wisdom."

The Leigh Perrots then had to accept the warden's hospitality until March when the trial would begin. What did they make of the strange charge that Aunt Jane faced? Her family has officially declared it to be the crude product of a blackmail conspiracy. William and Richard Arthur Austen-Leigh wrote in *Jane Austen, Her Life and Letters* (1913):

> There were also strong reasons for thinking that the accusation was the result of a deep-laid plot. Gye, the printer, who lived in the market-place, was believed to be the chief instigator. His character was indifferent, and he had money invested in Gregory's shop; and the business was in so bad a way that there was a temptation to seek for some large haul by way of blackmail. Mrs. Leigh Perrot was selected as the victim, people thought, because her husband was so extremely devoted to her that he would be sure to do anything to save her from the least vexation.

The trial took place on Saturday, March 29, at Taunton's Castle Hall, the scene of Judge Jeffreys's famous "Bloody Assize" in the seventeenth century. The hall, which seated 2,000, was filled to capacity, but Jane and Cassandra Austen were not among the audience. Aunt Jane, persisting in her desire to protect them from sharing her ordeal, wrote that she could not accept the offer of her nieces to attend—"to have two Young Creatures gazed at in a public Court would cut me to the very heart." The cast of legal participants in the trial was impressive. The judge, Sir Soulden Lawrence, had sat on the King's Bench since 1794 and had been a great friend of Samuel Johnson. The lead counsel for the prosecution was a future attorney general, Vicary Gibbs, K.C. Four able counsel acted for the defense, including a member of Parliament, Joseph Jekyll.

In his opening to the jury, Mr. Gibbs stated his anticipation that the defense would in all probability be either that Filby had by mistake enclosed the white lace in Mrs. Leigh Perrot's parcel, or that the case "was a malicious prosecution, set on foot for the purpose of extorting money from the Prisoner's husband." With respect to the latter possibility, Mr. Gibbs avowed: "If that be proved, there could not be a more infamous or wicked attempt. All the witnesses must, in that case, be perjured, and the crime would if possible be greater even than that wherewith the prisoner was charged." But Mr. Gibbs submitted that conspiracy could not be inferred from the conduct of the complainants

> who did not lie by to make the charge privately, but, on the contrary, immediately after the transaction, went to the Town-Hall, to lay information before the magistrates; and that, although many days elapsed . . . before the depositions could be taken, . . . yet they related all the circumstances to the town-clerk and deputy town-clerk, and to every person they met. It was then impossible to recall the report.

Elizabeth Gregory was the first witness called by the prosecution. She testified as to the arrangement of the shop premises. The shop was in the shape of a triangle, with its right wall perpendicular to Bath Street. As one entered from Bath Street, there was a counter along the right wall and a desk a little beyond it at the truncated rear angle of the shop. On the left hand there was another counter (of crucial importance in the case) which ran diagonally in the direction of the desk and parallel to the shop's left wall. Over the greater part of the length of the left counter (the portion closer to the rear of the shop and the desk) ran a brass railing, on which veils and handkerchiefs were hung. The distance from the shop entrance to the beginning of the brass rail was about two and a half yards and the rail itself was about two and a half yards long.

Miss Gregory recounted Mrs. Leigh Perrot's visit to the shop on August 8. When Mrs. Leigh Perrot asked to look again at the black lace she had examined the day before, Miss Gregory showed it to her. It was kept in a box on the left counter, in a space left clear by the rail at the end of the counter facing the back of the shop. Several veils and handkerchiefs hung down from the rail in such profusion as to obscure the view of any person behind them. Miss Gregory stood behind the counter with the left wall of the shop at her back, and Mrs. Leigh Perrot was in front of the counter. Mrs. Leigh Perrot decided on one of the several black laces that were in the box. While Miss Gregory was waiting on her customer, the clerk Filby was behind the counter, towards the end nearest the front of the shop, measuring white lace. According to Miss Gregory's testimony, she told Filby to measure the black lace she had just sold to Mrs. Leigh Perrot. Filby came down to the back end of the counter to perform that task and Miss Gregory then went to the desk and called to Miss Sarah Raines, her apprentice, to clear away the black lace box. Shortly Filby came to the desk and asked Miss Gregory for change for Mrs. Leigh Perrot's note. She gave him the change and then went downstairs to dinner, leaving Miss Raines at the desk.

Miss Gregory was in the downstairs kitchen when Filby came in and told her that he had observed Mrs. Leigh Perrot leaving the shop with a card of white lace. She testified that about ten minutes had passed between her having gone downstairs and her return to the shop floor. About a quarter of an hour later she spotted the Leigh Perrots on the street and accosted her customer, with the results already related. Miss Gregory stated that the paper parcel which Mrs. Leigh Perrot gave her at her request was "rumpled" and that the ends were both opened and not folded. She said that Mrs. Leigh Perrot "trembled very much, was much frightened, and coloured as red as scarlet." When Miss Gregory turned out a corner of the paper (in a manner she demonstrated to the Court) she saw a card of white lace, and the black lace over it. The black lace card was about an inch shorter than the white lace card beneath it. She saw her shop mark on the white lace card, and recognized that the mark was in Filby's handwriting.

On cross-examination, Miss Gregory testified that nobody came into the shop during the entire time Mrs. Leigh Perrot was there. Filby, she stated, was about six or seven yards from Mrs. Leigh Perrot when he stood at the forward end of the counter and was about four yards away from her when he measured and packed the lace at the back end of the counter. The witness testified that her customer was wearing a "black cloak."

The cross-examiner, Mr. Dallas, tried to probe the witness's testimony as to the timing of events following the alleged theft. Miss Gregory stated that she was in the kitchen for about ten minutes when Filby came to her with his story, and that she then immediately went up to the shop. This response was consistent with her testimony on direct examination,

PLAN of Miſs GREGORY's SHOP.
(Late WILLIAM SMITH's.)

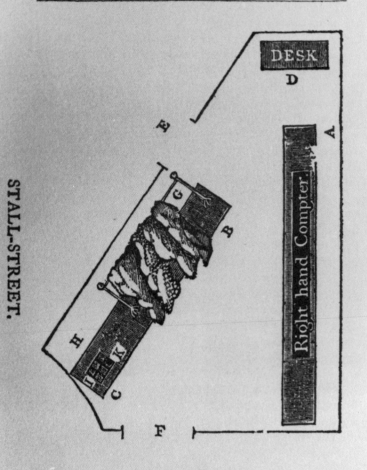

Plan of Miss Gregory's shop.

but she seemed to waver a bit as to the amount of time which then elapsed before she saw the Leigh Perrots on the street. Perhaps it was five minutes, but she could not exactly say how long it was, and, she added defensively, she never had since, at any moment, been able to say exactly what time had elapsed.

On re-examination, Miss Gregory clarified her earlier testimony by stating that nobody had *entered* the shop while Mrs. Leigh Perrot was there, but that "an old lady" had been there when Mrs. Leigh Perrot came in, and stayed about three minutes.

On a second cross-examination, Miss Gregory was questioned about her business relation with Mr. Gye and Mr. Lamb, the trustees for the creditors of her predecessor Mr. Smith, and she stated that she had purchased the shop from them on an installment basis and was carrying on business for her account. The cross-examiner was presumably hoping for testimony that Miss Gregory was in effect running the store for Smith or the trustees. However, it does not appear that she was asked a single question designed to elicit testimony in support of a claim that the trustee Mr. Gye was involved in a conspiracy against the Leigh Perrots.

Then the principal witness for the prosecution, Charles Filby, was called to the stand. He said that he had "lived with Miss Gregory as a shopman" for about six months prior to August 8. He had no prior experience in the millinery trade, and had twice been a bankrupt.

Filby remembered Mrs. Leigh Perrot's entering the shop. He could not recall that he had ever seen her before. When she came in, he was measuring white lace at the end of the left counter that was nearest the street. Standing behind the counter, he had the bottom part of the lace box on the right hand and the lid on his left. The lid contained the unmeasured lace folded on light blue cards. He took the lace from the cards, and having measured it put it on again, fixed a ticket to the lace noting the number of yards, and placed the measured lace in the bottom of the lace box on his right. Slightly contradicting Miss Gregory's testimony, he recalled that there was no other customer in the shop when Mrs. Leigh Perrot came in, but that a person came in afterwards, stayed four or five minutes, was served and went away.

Filby confirmed that Mrs. Leigh Perrot asked to be shown the lace she had seen the day before, and that Miss Gregory took down the black lace box for her at the back end of the counter. However, since he stood about four yards away, he had not heard the conclusion of the purchase when Miss Gregory called him over to measure the black lace her customer had selected. He had already put six measured cards of white lace in the bottom of the box. He particularly remembered the sixth card, because the original card had been worn so that he rewound the lace on a new card. When Miss Gregory called him, he was working on the seventh card, which he placed on top of the unmeasured pieces in the lid. He moved the lid to the seat where he had been sitting, and the bottom of the box remained on the counter.

Filby then went over to measure Mrs. Leigh Perrot's purchase at the farther end of the counter, while Sarah Raines put away the rest of the black lace. He wrapped Mrs. Leigh Perrot's lace round a small card. The witness showed how he then packed the lace in a piece of whited brown paper by holding it in the paper lengthwise, then turning inwards the two corners at each end to meet, and then doubling the ends down twice to make the parcel square. When he carried Mrs. Leigh Perrot's five-pound note to Miss Gregory at the desk four yards away, Filby said, his back was to the customer. As he turned around from the desk, he observed that Mrs. Leigh Perrot had moved from the place where he had left her to the other end of the counter and was facing the desk with her left hand towards the fatal box of white lace. As he was passing along the inside edge of the counter to deliver the change to her, his sight was obscured by the cascade of shawls and handkerchiefs, but when he emerged beyond the beginning of the railing, he saw Mrs. Leigh Perrot's "left hand come out of the box with a card of the lace in her hand." She drew her left hand under her cloak but Filby saw a corner of the blue card which the cloak did not conceal. Mrs. Leigh Perrot than took her departure as if she were one-armed. She held the purchased black lace in her right hand and then used the same hand to pick up the change which Filby had laid down on the counter.

Filby stated that he conversed with the two other shop assistants, Miss Raines and Miss Leeson, for about two or three minutes after Mrs. Leigh Perrot had left the shop, and then went downstairs to make his report to Miss Gregory. Although Filby said he did not examine the white lace box at this time, he swore positively that he had seen the customer remove the lace from the box.

After Miss Gregory recovered the lace, Filby went out to look for Mrs. Leigh Perrot and saw her and her husband turning the corner of the Abbey Churchyard. He asked Mr. Leigh Perrot's name, and was answered by that indignant husband "that he lived at No. 1, Paragon Buildings, and that his name was on the door." Filby went there directly and saw the name, and then went to Gye's, afterwards proceeding with Miss Gregory to the Town Hall in their first effort to present their complaint.

At the beginning of the cross-examination of Filby, the examiner, Mr. Bond, attempted to attack the witness's credibility by questions about his past business dealings and failures. Filby denied having had any dealings with a pawnbroker picturesquely named Crouch, but admitted his partnership with another man named Crout. With such a name in the firm, we are not surprised to read that, like an earlier enterprise in which Filby had engaged, the business went sour. Mr. Bond then asked whether Filby knew of an incident after August 8 in which a customer of the shop, Miss Blagrave, on her arrival home, found two veils in her parcel instead of the one she purchased from Filby. Filby said he did not know whether Miss Blagrave in fact found two veils in her package but admitted that she returned a veil the next morning and told him that he "ought to be very careful, considering what had lately happened with Mrs. Leigh Perrot." Reminded of his testimony on direct examination that he never wrapped more things than were purchased, Filby began to equivocate about Miss Blagrave. He did not know she was right, he was not obliged to believe her, he did not believe that he wrapped her purchase. He also denied knowledge of a woman named Kent coming to the shop a few days before Mrs. Leigh Perrot to complain about having received more gloves than she bought.

Mr. Bond then turned to the witness's testimony with respect to the alleged theft. Filby stated that, upon coming back and looking in the box of white lace, he found a vacancy in the left corner of the box where he had put the last measured card of lace (the new card). When he saw the defendant's left hand in the box, only Miss Raines and Miss Leeson were in the shop, Miss Raines busy with needlework at the rear of the shop and Miss Leeson behind some muslin at the rear of the shop with her back to the defendant.

Counsel failed to shake Filby's testimony that he not only saw Mrs. Leigh Perrot's hand in the box but also saw the card in her hand under her cloak. He was quite certain she was wearing a cloak: "Prisoner had on a black mode cloak . . . it was not a long cloak, but one that reached just below her elbows. . . ."

Filby testified that the distance from Paragon Buildings (where the Leigh Perrots lived) to the shop on Bath Street was about a quarter of a mile, and conceded that he "[did not] know but that there was time to have gone home if she had chosen to do so." He stated that he stayed in the downstairs kitchen about four or five minutes after he reported the theft to Miss Gregory, and when he came back up into the shop he met Miss Gregory with the recovered card of lace in her hand.

On re-examination, Filby said he was certain that from the time he went to serve Mrs. Leigh Perrot at the back end of the counter he had never been nearer to the place where the white lace was left.

Sarah Raines was then called to testify. She confirmed the prior testimony as to the places where the defendant, Miss Gregory, and Filby were during the transaction. She saw Filby measure the purchased black lace and wrap it in paper and that there was nothing else in the paper. She added that Filby did not move from her side while she was putting away the rest of the black lace, that he was not half a yard away from her, and that before she left Filby when he was about to deliver the parcel to the defendant, Filby and she were about four yards from the white lace box.

On cross-examination by Mr. Jekyll, she admitted that "there was nothing particular to draw her attention in the manner of Filby's putting up the black lace, and that she sees him every day putting up parcels— that she did not then pay any particular attention to him, nor did she observe particularly from whence he took the paper to wrap up the parcel in. . . ."

Following these admissions, the Judge asked the witness his own questions to test her evidence that there was no white lace in the package:

Q. You say he did not put any white lace in the parcel with the black; how could you know that not being particularly observant?

A. I saw that he put in the black lace only.

Q. Are you certain of that?

A. Yes, my lord, I am.

The prosecution closed its case, and it was now the turn of the defense. The opportunities for the defense were severely limited under the criminal procedure of the time. The defendant could not testify in her own behalf nor could her husband testify in her defense. The defendant was permitted to make an unsworn statement. Mrs. Leigh Perrot attempted to address the Court, but "after speaking a few sentences she became so much agitated that her voice failed her," and Mr. Jekyll was requested to repeat her address as dictated to him by his client. The address was brief and stressed Mrs. Leigh Perrot's lack of motive:

Placed in a situation the most eligible that any woman could desire, with supplies so ample that I was left rich after every wish was gratified—blessed in the affections of the most generous man as a husband, what could induce me to commit such a crime? Depraved indeed must that mind be that under such circumstances could be so culpable.

Mrs. Leigh Perrot's statement also advertised the evidence as to her conduct and character that would be given by her "noble and truly respectable friends," but asserted that she would make no comment on the evidence against her. She did permit herself one remark on what she believed to be a weakness in the prosecution's case: "I will only ask you whether to be found opposite to the Shop within the space of little more than half an hour, and with the Lace in my hand is like the conduct of a Guilty Person."

The defense then put on its case. The pawnbroker Mr. Crouch had been located in Cripplegate, London. He testified that Filby and his brother had done business in haberdashery goods at his house six or seven years before, but believed that the witness Charles Filby "might not have been with him on business more than once."

Miss Blagrave then gave her account of the superfluous veil as to which Filby had been questioned. She said that she had purchased and paid for one veil at Smith's shop on September 19, and received her package from a "tall shopman" whom she identified as Filby. When she opened the parcel at home she found a second veil which she returned to Filby the next day. He remembered waiting on her, took the veil and thanked her, saying that he had not missed it. On cross-examination, the witness said she did not know Mrs. Leigh Perrot and had never been accused of stealing the veil.

Mrs. Mary Kent was put on the stand to testify as to another case of alleged negligent wrapping at the Smith shop. She had purchased four pairs of gloves at the shop in August and had found five in her parcel. She was not sure who served her but thought it was "Mrs. Smith's sister" (Miss Gregory).

The defense then led on a procession of distinguished witnesses as to Mrs. Leigh Perrot's fine conduct, character, reputation and religious principles, and—last but not least—Mr. Leigh Perrot's reputation as a man of considerable property. The fourteen witnesses included George Vansittart and Francis Annesby, members of Parliament for Berkshire and Reading; Lord Braybroke; Rev. Mr. Nind, vicar of Wargrave, in Berkshire (the parish where the Leigh Perrots' house was situated); and Rev. Mr. Wake, curate of the Bath parish. A linen draper, a mercer, and a jeweler, all from Bath, testified unanimously as to Mrs. Leigh Perrot's honest dealings in three separate lines of commerce.

The defense then rested, and the judge summed up the evidence for the jury. The jury then retired, and after fifteen minutes returned with a verdict of "not guilty."

Despite the happy outcome, Mrs. Leigh Perrot was a severe critic of the trial. In a letter to a cousin on April 1, 1800, she gave mixed ratings to the judge and her counsel. She praised Mr. Justice Lawrence's politeness but opined that: "he did not let enough be said of Filby's Villainy—he thought enough had been said to fully clear me, and was pretty sure that the winding up of his Charge to the Jury would put every doubt respecting my Innocence out of the Question; but I think it was a dangerous Experiment. She was disappointed in the performance of two of her counsel but thought one of them made up for forensic deficiencies by a real talent for sobbing. She regretted that neither her husband nor she was permitted to give evidence under oath, "else I could have disproved my having on any Cloak, tho the Villain swore he saw the lace *under my black Cloak*." She did not, however, explain why she made no mention of her attire in her unsworn statement to the court.

What are we to make, with the hindsight of two centuries, of the merits of the case against Jane's aunt?

Sir Frank Douglas MacKinnon, in his book on the case, *Grand Larceny* (1937), does not analyze the nature and quality of the evidence at the trial. He was content to reprint verbatim a contemporary account of the proceedings "taken in court" by John Pinchard, an attorney at Taunton, and to let that record speak for itself. MacKinnon's reticence is not surprising since his book drew in large part on previously unpublished correspondence to which he was given access by the Austen-Leigh family. For him to have suggested, even by pausing to weigh evidence, that there would be any basis for doubting the tradition of conspiracy against Aunt Jane would not have been regarded by the family as an act of gratitude. Therefore, it may be worth an effort to take a closer look at the evidence on the principal issues of the case.

Was there a conspiracy to extort money from the Leigh Perrots?

It was the strong belief of the Leigh Perrots, which is accepted without question in Jane Austen biographies, that the case against Aunt Jane was trumped up in the belief that James Leigh Perrot could be induced to pay a large sum of money to spare his wife from imprisonment and trial. In fact, the tradition continues, the conspirators failed because the Leigh Perrots refused to yield to extortion and instead weathered the judicial ordeal together.

The prosecutor in the trial pointed out one of the difficulties with the conspiracy theory. The parties who initiated the prosecution did not make the charge privately to the Leigh Perrots but, immediately after the recovery of the white lace, went to the Town Hall to lay their charge before the magistrates. Even though many days elapsed before their depositions could be taken, Miss Gregory and Filby gave the matter as much publicity as they could in the meantime, relating the circumstances to the town clerk and his deputy and to every person in town who was willing to listen to them. They would have found it very difficult to retract the charges if they had been motivated by blackmail or indeed even if they had believed themselves in the right but wished to leave the door open to financial redress.

It is an assumption of the conspiracy theory that the ringleader,

William Gye, had marked out the Leigh Perrots as victims in advance because James was known to be wealthy and deeply devoted to his wife. If this assumption is worthy of belief, then it is only reasonable to suppose that Gye and his confederates would have known the Leigh Perrots by sight and would also have known their home address. However, it was the testimony of Filby, unchallenged on cross-examination, that after the occurrence at the store he had gone looking for the Leigh Perrots and had asked them their names. When an annoyed Mr. Leigh Perrot gave him his address and told him to look for his name on the door, Filby lost no time in doing precisely as he was told. He noted the name, went to Gye's, and afterwards went with Miss Gregory to the Town Hall. Unless Filby was engaged in some rather pointless playacting, it very much appears that he had made an effort to confirm the identity of the Leigh Perrots for the purpose of enabling Miss Gregory to provide proper information in laying her charge with the magistrates.

In support of the family tradition of a blackmail plot, the Austen-Leighs showed Sir Frank Douglas MacKinnon certain anonymous letters purportedly sent to the Leigh Perrots by two people claiming to have overheard Gye and his confederates plotting their villainy. Although the two letters are signed with different initials and apparently are written in different hands, they have such strong stylistic similarities as to suggest that they were dictated by a single source. Both writers claim to have been employees of Gye. The first, who wrote on February 12, 1800 to Mr. Leigh Perrot, makes the self-serving statement that "had I the means of *gaining Bread for my Family* in any honest way I should gladly leave an employment under as malicious & vile a Man as ever existed" (emphasis added). The second writer, who sent his letter to Mr. Leigh Perrot on a date which looks like October 29, expressed similar discontent with the way he earned his "bread": "I am obliged to *earn Bread for a large Family* in any honest manner I can; and although it is my hard lot *to get that Bread* in the employment of one of the greatest Rascals that ever lived, I have the conscious pleasure of knowing that I have more than once been of service to those who might have suffered from his dishonesty" (emphasis added).

In addition to these anonymous letters, the Leigh Perrots received another letter from a friend in Bath, Daniel Lysons, which indicates that there was talk of the Gye conspiracy in the higher social circles of Bath as well. Presumably these letters were shown by the Leigh Perrots to their lawyers, who would have had an opportunity to investigate the rumors and to focus their inquiries on the employees of Gye. We do not know whether any such investigation was undertaken, but we are left with this curious result, that the only reference in the trial, as recounted by Mr.

Pinchard, to the possibility of a blackmail plot was made by the prosecutor in his opening statement to the jury. Of course, his effort was to induce the jury to discount that possibility, which might have been implanted in their minds by local gossip. However, absolutely no evidence was introduced by the defense to suggest the existence of a blackmail plot, and, instead, the defense was squarely based on the theory that the white lace was inadvertently enclosed in Mrs. Leigh Perrot's package through the negligence of the clerk Filby.

In fact, one of the circumstances that was principally relied on by the defense to demonstrate Aunt Jane's innocence proves still more definitively that there was no conspiracy against her. I refer to her being found on the street across from Smith's with the white lace in her possession about a half hour after she left the shop. Surely, if the object of the plot had been to find her with the incriminating lace on her person, Filby or Miss Gregory would have immediately pursued her as she left the premises and recovered the lace as soon as she moved far enough to accomplish what the common-law experts with their "little Latin" liked to call "asportation" (carrying away). Such apprehensions were not uncommon in the eighteenth century, as evidenced by the following account:

> We had not been long out of the shop but the mercer missed the piece of stuff, and sent his messengers, one one way, and one another, and they presently seized her that had the piece; as for me, I had very luckily stepped into a house . . . and had the satisfaction, or the terror, indeed, of looking out of the window, and seeing the poor creature dragged away to the justice, who immediately committed her to Newgate.

In these words Daniel Defoe's famous shoplifter Moll Flanders describes the capture of her confederate.

But the supposed conspirators of the William Smith millinery shop did not set out in hot pursuit of Aunt Jane. How did they know, then, that she would conveniently return to the neighborhood a half hour later with the missing lace still in the original package, however "rumpled"? They could not have known. The recovery of the lace was fortuitous, and the conspiracy theory is apparently a fantasy.

Did Filby perjure himself in testifying that Mrs. Leigh Perrot hid the stolen lace under her black cloak?

As noted, Mrs. Leigh Perrot complained bitterly that, due to her husband's legal incapacity to testify in her behalf, she had been unable to disprove the testimony of the clerk Filby that she had hidden the black lace under her "black cloak." She maintained that she was not wearing a cloak at all, and that Filby was lying. However, it would be hard to believe that the Leigh Perrots, promenading on one of the main streets

of Bath where they were well known, did not come across a single friend
or acquaintance on the day in question who could have testified that
Mrs. Leigh Perrot was not wearing a cloak. No such testimony was
introduced. Filby would have been taking a great risk in lying about
Mrs. Leigh Perrot's apparel, since the possibility of the defense's producing a contradictory witness should have struck him as very great
indeed.

How persuasive was the evidence that Filby included the white lace in
Mrs. Leigh Perrot's package through negligence?

In support of its theory that Filby inadvertently wrapped the white
lace in Mrs. Leigh Perrot's package, the defense tried to establish that
both the Smith millinery shop and Filby were negligent wrappers.
Evidence of two other instances of similar "mistakes" was introduced,
Miss Blagrave's testimony as to the veils and Mrs. Mary Kent's as to the
gloves. The judge, in his instructions to the jury, allowed the Blagrave
evidence to stand, since she identified Filby as the wrapper, but he
instructed the jury to disregard the Kent testimony since it appeared that
she had been served by some woman in the shop.

Although under Anglo-American evidentiary rules evidence of negligent "habits" can be introduced in support of an effort to show an act of
negligence in a particular instance, one subsequent mistake in wrapping
on Filby's part does not appear to go very far in dispelling the force of
the prosecution's evidence against Mrs. Leigh Perrot. This appears with
particular force when the physical circumstances of the Blagrave incident are contrasted with the uncontroverted testimony in the Leigh
Perrot case. If Filby in fact packed two veils for Miss Blagrave instead of
the one she bought, it is likely that he drew the second veil from the same
box or counter area from which he took the veil she had selected.
However, the white lace discovered in Mrs. Leigh Perrot's package had
been wound on a card at a location approximately *four yards* away from
the area where Filby packed Mrs. Leigh Perrot's purchased black lace. If
Filby made the error in packing which the defense attributed to him, he
would have had to carry a card of white lace for the distance of four
yards and to place it on the counter before him or hold it in his hand
while he proceeded to wind Mrs. Leigh Perrot's lace and prepare her
package. This "mistake" would have involved a degree of somnambu-
lism (and possibly manual dexterity) on the part of Filby that is hardly
to be compared with the alleged miscounting of Miss Blagrave's veils.

Do the circumstances of the discovery of the white lace in the posses-
sion of Mrs. Leigh Perrot support the negligence theory by proving her
lack of consciousness of guilt?

The judge seems to have been clearly correct in discounting the prosecution's evidence that Mrs. Leigh Perrot, when accosted in the street by Miss Gregory, was agitated and had "turned as red as scarlet," nor should we have been surprised had she turned white as lace. The court observed that the defendant's reaction should not:

> be construed by them [the jury] into an indication of guilt for that, if any person were to be suddenly stopped in the public street, and taxed with the commission of so heinous a crime, such a charge, however conscious of innocence the party might be, would, in all probability, be productive of effects similar to those described by the witness.

I think, however, that some quarrel could be taken with his lordship's accentuation of the defense argument that Mrs. Leigh Perrot's "returning and passing by the shop, with the parcel containing the lace in her hand, so soon after she had left it, when it was proved by the witness Filby that sufficient time had elapsed for her to have gone home and concealed it, had she chosen so to do, certainly did not appear to be the conduct of a guilty person, for that thieves are wont to hide away and conceal the property they have stolen."

I have already argued that the fortuitous reappearance of Aunt Jane tends to undermine the notion that the recovery of the lace was the result of a "deep-laid" conspiracy. But could the circumstances of the recovery, by evidencing Aunt Jane's lack of guilty awareness, tend to support the alternative theory (on which the defense in court was based) that the white lace was included in Aunt Jane's parcel by negligence? It was common ground that Aunt Jane's residence at 1 Paragon Buildings was only a quarter of a mile away from the shop and that she would have had time to return home to hide the incriminating white lace. This, however, is at best a very ambiguous factor. There is no evidence as to what Mrs. Leigh Perrot's destination was after her famous visit to the millinery shop. It is possible that she did not enter the shop with any theft in mind and had already arranged to meet her husband in town at a fixed hour and place that would not have permitted a prior return home. Why, then, could she not have said to the doting Uncle James when she met him that she desired to walk along home with him so that she could leave off a package? Perhaps it was because the package was small, and James, afflicted with gout, was a painful walker.

As to Uncle James's sorry condition only two months earlier we can summon Jane Austen herself as witness. In her letter of June 2 she wrote to Cassandra, "My uncle overwalked himself at first, and can now only travel in a chair, but is otherwise very well."

What weight is to be given to Mrs. Leigh Perrot's social position and character evidence?

It appears quite likely that Mrs. Leigh Perrot's speedy acquittal was due less to defects in the prosecution's proof than to the great weight accorded by the court and the jury to Mrs. Leigh Perrot's social position and character evidence. The question ultimately came down to this: Is it believable that a woman of Mrs. Leigh Perrot's wealth and position with a fine character testified to by neighbors and friends of high birth and standing, by clergymen from two parishes, and by three merchants from Bath, would have committed a disgraceful shoplifting? Mr. Justice Lawrence in summing up the evidence to the jury laid heavy stress on the testimony as to Mrs. Leigh Perrot's good character. Before turning to that evidence, he observed to the jury that "the case on the part of the prosecution was fully proved, if they believed the testimony of the witnesses called in support of it." He commented that as to the good character of Filby "there hung some doubt," but he concluded that "the evidence given by him stood uncontradicted except in one point of trivial consequence, namely, his having sworn that he never had any dealings with Crouch, the pawnbroker, whereas it afterwards appears from Crouch's evidence that Filby was *once* or perhaps twice at his house on business, which was eight or nine years ago." He particularly pointed out the corroboration of Filby's evidence by the testimony of Miss Gregory and her apprentice Sarah Raines and pointed out that Miss Raines had sworn positively that she took particular notice of Filby's putting up a parcel of black lace and that there was nothing but the black lace put into it by him.

The judge, however, thought it very persuasive that no person could have received a higher character from more distinguished witnesses than had Mrs. Leigh Perrot and concluded, "If upon taking all the circumstances of the case into consideration, the Jury should see any reason to disbelieve the witnesses for the prosecution, or which led them to doubt of the Prisoner's guilt, they should recollect the very excellent character which had been given her, and in that case it ought to have great weight with them towards an acquittal." These were his lordship's concluding words. The jury must have been impressed by this instruction, which reinforced the point made by the defendant's counsel in the address he had read to the court at her dictation. It seems obvious, then, that despite the long-lived tradition that Mrs. Leigh Perrot was freed because conspirators clumsily failed to impose perjured testimony on the court and jury, the outcome turned instead on the jury's disbelief that a rich and respectable woman would have committed a minor theft.

Unfortunately, lawyers who have had to struggle in modern days with the defense of retail establishments against shoplifting losses and false arrest charges know that rich and respectable women *do* commit thefts even of the most trivial kind, and that shoplifting is often an irrational crime. What the emotional roots of such crimes may be remains a puzzle. It is possible that one source of middle-class shoplifting may be a warped sense of economy, a revolt, conscious or unconscious, against high prices. Could such feelings as this have impelled the affluent Mrs. Leigh Perrot to steal the white lace? Since the biographical data about her have been in the hands of the family, we have very little insight into her foibles. However, the family biographers William and Richard Arthur Austen-Leigh confide that "she was not exactly open-handed." An intriguing possibility may be built on this hint. We will recall from Jane Austen's letters that millinery prices in Bath were high. We also know that Mrs. Leigh Perrot, on the day before the incident, had been in the Smith shop examining some black lace from London. Only on a second visit had she brought herself to conclude the purchase and perhaps she regarded the price as extravagant. It is therefore possible that when she saw the opportunity of taking the white lace, she acted, like the stock investors of our time, to "average down" her purchase price.

Other affluent shoplifters appear to have been motivated by elements in their family relations that are not on public view. As an example I might cite the recent story, *A Case of Shoplifting* by Michael Gilbert (1976). I suspect that Michael Gilbert, as a lawyer, has more than a little familiarity with apparently inexplicable shopliftings. In his story, Gilbert tells of Mrs. Kent-Smith, the wife of a busy self-made business tycoon, who simulates a shoplifting (and an intentionally unsuccessful one at that) for the purpose of attracting her husband's attention. We are told that the Leigh Perrots were a devoted couple, but a wife's notion of the degree of attention to which she is entitled does not necessarily coincide with the views of outside observers. Of course, since shoplifting was a capital offense, it would have been a dangerous form of attention-getting. Nevertheless, in light of the enormous volume of shoplifting in eighteenth-century England, there is little reason to believe that capital punishment acted as more of a deterrent to this offense than it did to more serious crimes.

It is risky to attempt to descend to lower levels of Mrs. Leigh Perrot's psyche since we know so little about her. Michael Gilbert, who could take greater liberties with his fictional Mrs. Kent-Smith, stressed her childlessness. Perhaps Mr. Gilbert was bowing in the direction of the theory espoused by Freudian psychiatrists that an adult female shoplifter acting from no apparent economic motive is often a childless woman who compensates for her deprivation of children by taking things belonging to others. Whether the childless Mrs. Leigh Perrot might have fit this pattern we cannot know.

It is hard enough to convince a modern jury that shoplifting may have other than economic motives. It is possible that in Taunton in 1800 it would have been significantly harder to make the point that rich people not classically "mad" might be guilty of a petty theft. In the principal contemporary authority on crime and its prevention, P. Colquhoun's *Treatise on the Police of the Metropolis*, which was first published in London in 1795, a purely economic theory of the origin of petty theft is propounded. In Colquhoun's view, the principal explanation of theft was that the poor class was tempted to commit this crime because of the existence of specialized dealers in the various categories of stolen goods, ranging from metals to second-hand apparel. His proposed solution was the close supervision of these trading markets.

Ironically, however, the files of the Austen-Leigh family themselves contain some evidence of contemporary insight into the possibility of irrational shoplifting. The source once again is an anonymous letter-writer. In a letter to Mrs. Leigh Perrot of April 20, 1800 the female writer offered to act as an intermediary "to prevent the publishing of a scandalous print which discovered by accident is now in a forward state the subject of which is the crest of Mr. Leigh Perrot with a card of lace in the bill of the Parrot with other things and an inscription referring to the late accusation which was made against you." The writer claimed to have been authorized by the printmakers (who merited prosecution not only for extortion but also for their execrable pun on the Perrot name) to offer the withdrawal of the print in exchange for a subscription of one hundred guineas to a city hospital which was in arrears. Professing a belief in Mrs. Leigh Perrot's innocence, the correspondent attributed to the publishers of the print a resolution "to lend their aid to punish you lest a sufficient impression should not yet be made on the mind of yourself & (as they were pleased to express themselves) other *genteel shoplifters*" (emphasis added).

We do not have any direct record of Jane Austen's reactions to her aunt's trial. In her novels Jane Austen became the mistress of the art of piercing the veil of "first impressions," which enabled her, for example, to unmask the hidden immorality of two gentlemen, Mr. Wickham in *Pride and Prejudice* and Mr. Elliot in *Persuasion*. But Jane surely must have believed that her aunt was innocent. It is harder to have insight within the family.

There is no direct translation of Mrs. Leigh Perrot's ordeal in Jane Austen's fiction. It is in keeping with the character of a writer whose novels reflect only obliquely the wars and public events of her time that she should not have chosen to work the raw materials of a family criminal trial. However, a close look at the two Bath novels of Jane Austen, *Northanger Abbey* and *Persuasion*, may give us glimpses of Aunt Jane and memories of her day in court.

In *Northanger Abbey* (which may have been first written in 1798 and revised about 1803) the heroine, seventeen-year-old Catherine Morland, is taken to Bath by Mr. and Mrs. Allen, a childless couple who are friends of her family. Although Jane Austen drew no characters wholly from life, there are a number of parallels between Jane and Catherine, and between the Leigh Perrots and the Allens. By the time of the composition of *Northanger Abbey*, Jane, who like Catherine Morland was a minister's daughter, had visited the childless Leigh Perrots in Bath. Mr. Allen like Mr. Leigh Perrot took the waters of Bath as a cure for his gout. Although Mrs. Leigh Perrot appears to have had a more dour personality than Mrs. Allen, it is possible that the acute young Jane saw in her aunt aspects of Mrs. Allen's dominant trait, a passion for clothes and a compulsive need to surpass all her acquaintances in finery. Mrs. Allen's deepest emotion on crossing the crowded floor of the Upper Assembly Rooms is self-congratulation on having preserved her gown from injury: " 'It would have been very shocking to have it torn,' said she, 'would not it? It is such a delicate muslin. For my part, I have not seen anything I like so well in the whole room, I assure you.' " And she interrupts her expression of concern about her failure to get Catherine a partner with a comment on a dress in the crowd: "There goes a strange-looking woman! What an odd gown she has got on! How old-fashioned it is! Look at the back." When she meets her childhood friend Mrs. Thorpe, she is delighted to discover with her keen eyes that "the lace on Mrs. Thorpe's pelisse was not half so handsome as that on her own."

Perhaps a passion such as this drove Mrs. Leigh Perrot into the millinery shops of Bath. She may have agreed with Mrs. Allen's judgment of the attractions of the town for shoppers: "Bath is a charming place, sir; there are so many good shops here. We are sadly off in the country. . . . Now, here one can step out of doors, and get a thing in five minutes."

The concluding portion of *Persuasion*, Jane Austen's last completed novel (published in 1818) is also set in Bath. Here very clear imprints of Jane's memories of her aunt's trial appear. It may be mere accident that in this novel there are more references to law and lawyers than are customary in the Austen novels. The early chapters introduce Mr. Shepherd, "a civil, cautious lawyer," one of the few portraits drawn by Jane Austen from his profession. Later in the book, when Mrs. Smith reveals to Anne Elliot the evidence she has preserved of the treachery of Anne's unwanted suitor, the self-seeking Mr. Elliot, she speaks like a barrister addressing a jury: "I have shown you Mr. Elliot as he was a dozen years ago, and I will show him as he is now. I cannot produce written proof again, but I can give as authentic oral testimony as you can desire, of what he is now wanting, and what he is now doing."

Whether or not these associations of law with the town of Bath are related to recollection of Mrs. Leigh Perrot's case, other allusions in the book are unmistakably connected with the trial. Mr. Shepherd receives an application for tenancy of Kellynch Hall from Admiral Croft "with whom he afterwards fell into company in attending the quarter sessions at Taunton," the town where Aunt Jane was tried. Later we learn that Mr. Musgrove "always attends the assizes, and I am so glad when they are over, and he is safe back again." Perhaps Anne Elliot's dislike of Bath mirrors Jane Austen's feelings toward a town that was associated with two family tragedies, the death of her father and the criminal charge against her aunt.

The conclusion of *Persuasion* presents final proof that the trial of Aunt Jane left a lasting impression on the mind of her famous niece. Dissatisfied with chapter 10 of her original version of *Persuasion*, which reunited Anne Elliot and Captain Wentworth in a rather tepid drawing room scene, Jane Austen expanded and relocated the final episodes of their reconciliation. In a key scene of the revised version, Anne's sister Mary, looking out of a window of the White Hart in Stall Street, sees a woman standing under the colonnade with a gentleman she identifies as Mr. Elliot. She "saw them turn the corner from Bath Street just now."

On that very corner stood the shop where Aunt Jane had her unhappy encounter with a card of white lace.

Gilbert and Sullivan on Corporation Law: *Utopia, Limited* and the Panama Canal Frauds

If the name Gilbert is mentioned to the president of a modern corporation he is likely to think of the brothers Lewis and John and to wonder what shareholder proposals they may be preparing for the forthcoming annual meeting. However, the title of corporate gadfly extraordinary could with equal justice be awarded to quite another Gilbert, W. S. Gilbert of the operatic partnership of Gilbert and Sullivan. In the relatively little-known opera, *Utopia, Limited*, which appeared at the Savoy Theatre in 1893, Gilbert delivered a sharply satirical assault on business corporations (which the English call "companies"), and particularly on the basic corporate concept of limited liability. The opera sketches the development of a utopian society that organizes itself, its ruler, and all of its citizens as limited liability companies under the English Companies Act of 1862.

The theme of *Utopia, Limited* has puzzled its critics and received strange evaluations. W. A. Darlington, in his *The World of Gilbert and Sullivan* (1950) makes the suggestion (which he cautiously terms a guess) that "Gilbert, not being in any sense a businessman, had never had any clear notion what a limited-liability company was" until shortly before he wrote *Utopia*. In the light of his celebrated partnership disputes with Sullivan, Gilbert may be denied a businessman's standing only under the most subjective conception of that calling, but surely Darlington would not have us forget that the author of *Utopia* was a lawyer.

It is apparent from Hesketh Pearson's description in *Gilbert: His Life and Strife* (1957) that Gilbert's career at the bar was spectacularly unsuccessful. It lasted four years, produced about twenty clients and a total income of £100. His difficulties seem to be fairly represented by his first brief, the defense of a female pickpocket, who, upon being sentenced to a prison term, "threw a boot at his head and continued to criticize his personal character until removed from the court." The memories of this case are undoubtedly responsible for Gilbert's little gem, the short story, *My Maiden Brief.* In that story, the fledgling barrister, Horace Penditton, prepares for the trial of his first client, who filched a purse on an omnibus, by trying out a fanciful line of defense on Felix Polter, a barrister who occupies neighboring chambers in the Inner Temple. When Penditton appears in court, he is shocked to find that his opponent is none other than Polter, who calmly proceeds to anticipate all his defenses in opening the prosecution's case to the jury. When Penditton at the end of the story contrasts Polter's future with his own, we may be hearing a *cri de coeur* of Gilbert himself: "He is now a flourishing Old Bailey counsel, while I am as briefless as ever."

Although Gilbert's years as a lawyer were few, he had a very active and lifelong career as a client. In addition to his disputes with Sullivan and D'Oyly Carte over the expense of new carpets at the Savoy Theatre, and a defamation suit against a newspaper, he filled his private hours with threats of litigation over grievances real and trivial. If his correspondence with an adversary took an unsatisfactory turn, he was likely to suggest that future letters be addressed to his solicitor. However, it is to his credit that he saw the world of the law whole by rounding out his functions as lawyer and client with able and compassionate service as a justice of the peace.

It is odd that neither Gilbert's contemporaries nor his biographers seem to have taken him seriously as a critic of business law and morality. Doubt seems always to arise as to whether Gilbert had strong roots in the real world. Of course, we have always enjoyed the game of matching Gilbert characters with eminent and lesser Victorians, but there has been no agreement that Gilbert was engaged by the social issues that enveloped the individual figures he found suitable for caricature. His biographer, Hesketh Pearson, ventures a psychological explanation for Gilbert's preoccupation with fairyland and fantasy. Pearson believes that Gilbert's childhood spent with incompatible and often feuding parents left him "an internal discomfort, a desire to see things as they are not, born of his early contact with an unpleasant actuality." Gilbert, on the other hand, had a perfectly pragmatic justification for his specialization in fairies. In his fairy tale, *The Wicked World*, he explained his choice of theme. He did not write of fashionable life because he knew nothing of fashion; nor did he write a medieval romance because this would require too much research (which Gilbert detested and preferred to call "cramming"). Gilbert noted the possible objection by an acute reader that if the author knew nothing of fashionable life, he must know still less about fairies. He offered a reply that is unanswerable: "Exactly. I know nothing at all about fairies—but then neither do you."

Perhaps the fantastic settings of Gilbert's plots have obscured his interest in legal issues. In some instances the reluctance of drama critics and audiences to listen to his more serious voice impeded his forays into criticism of prevailing legal principles. This was clearly his fate when he attempted to deal in his works with controversies in the field of criminal law. In Gilbert and Sullivan's *Iolanthe*, as first performed in 1882, the young shepherd Strephon, on admission to Parliament, delivered a speech attributing crime to circumstances of birth and upbringing:

> Take a wretched thief
> Through the City sneaking,
> Pocket handkerchief
> Ever, ever seeking:
> What is he but I
> Robbed of all my chances—
> Picking pockets by
> Force of circumstances?
> I might be as bad—
> As unlucky, rather—
> If I'd only had
> Fagin for a father!

Leslie Baily in his admirable *Gilbert & Sullivan Book* (1952) notes that the critic of the *London Times* attacked Gilbert's expression of anger, "a passion altogether out of place in a 'fairy opera.' " The offending song was later cut from *Iolanthe*.

Gilbert's final dramatic work, the one-act play *The Hooligan*, produced in 1911, the last year of his life, was a completely serious treatment of capital punishment. Inspired by his fascination with the celebrated Crippen murder trial of 1910, Gilbert's play presented the last moments of a condemned murderer in his prison cell. The criminal is reprieved from hanging only to die of heart failure occasioned by the agony of waiting for death. Some of the spectators who expected laughs from Gilbert were puzzled and hissed.

Gilbert's literary reflection of his interest in criminal law is pretty much limited to the two examples given above (unless we are also to refer to his portrait of that great penologist, the Mikado of Japan). However, throughout the pages of his opera librettos are many signs of his perennial absorption in the behavior of corporations and businessmen. It is likely that his contemporaries cared as little for his views on business as they did for his principles of criminal law. If we are to follow their pattern by assuming that Gilbert's comments on business morality have no application to our own time, we will probably be drawing upon some false feeling of comfort.

Gilbert's first satire on corporations appeared appropriately in the very first opera he wrote with Sullivan, *Thespis*. In this opera, Thespis, the manager of a theatrical troupe performing for the Olympian gods, sings the first Gilbert and Sullivan patter song about the chairman of a railroad's board of directors who undermined his own authority and ruined his company by being too affable to company employees. I suppose that even the most democratic of executives would feel that the chairman went to extremes in his personnel policy:

> Each Christmas Day he gave each stoker
> A silver shovel and a golden poker,
> He'd button-hole flowers for the ticket sorters,
> And rich Bath-buns for the outside porters.
> He'd mount the clerks on his first-class hunters,
> And he built little villas for the road-side shunters,
> And if any were fond of pigeon shooting,
> He'd ask them down to his place at Tooting.

The employees, surprised by the chairman's favors, assumed that his behavior was due to an odd quirk of humor rather than generosity, and attempted to respond in kind by diverting any train on which he happened to be riding. The employees' vein of practical joking appeared to please the chairman more than the railroad's customers or shareholders:

> This pleased his whim and seemed to strike it,
> But the general public did not like it,
> The receipts fell, after a few repeatings,
> And he got it hot at the annual meetings . . .

Undeterred by shareholder pressure, the chairman continued to indulge the employees in their merry pranks, with the result of business failure for himself and the investors:

> The shareholders are all in the work'us [workhouse],
> And he sells pipe-lights in the Regent Circus.

The first corporation song of Gilbert's is obviously less concerned with business practice than with an important tenet of Gilbert's conservative personality, namely, that excessive egalitarianism is fatal to established order. However, the song of Thespis also reveals two points that are crucial to an understanding of Gilbert's lasting interest in corporations. The lyrics show first his tendency to relate observations on corporate administration with theatrical management, a field in which he was to spend his life and where he was to encounter a great deal of difficulty in reconciling the conflicting interests of manager, investor and employee. A second characteristic theme that the early song shows in germination is Gilbert's emphasis on the responsibility of corporate management to the public, including those whose investments they have called upon and those with whom they do business.

Eleven years later in Gilbert's great libretto for *Iolanthe*, business practice had become the stuff of nightmare, though of a comic turn. The lord chancellor, in his celebrated nightmare aria, recalls a dream in which a distinctly small fellow with a Protean inclination to change identities harangues a group of sailors on a new financing he is pushing. The promoter, who appears successively as an attorney and an eleven-year-old boy, describes the purpose of the financing in terms which are recalled by the delirious chancellor as follows:

> It's a scheme of devices, to get at low prices all goods from cough mixtures to cables
> (Which tickled the sailors), by treating retailers as though they were all vege*ta*bles—
> You get a good spadesman to plant a small tradesman (first take off his boots with a boot-tree),
> And his legs will take root, and his fingers will shoot, and they'll blossom and bud like a fruit-tree—
> From the greengrocer tree you get grapes and green pea, cauliflower, pineapple, and cranberries,
> While the pastrycook plant cherry brandy will grant, apple puffs, and three-corners, and Banburys—
> The shares are a penny, and ever so many are taken by Rothschild and Baring,
> And just as a few are allotted to you, you awake with a shudder despairing.

Only the timely waking of the chancellor has saved him from a disastrous investment. However, in spite of our regulatory advances, the sales techniques of the undersized promoter are not unlike those of present-day "penny stock" merchants, in whose sales pitch the projected use of proceeds may be less important than the general impression that the venture is new and that, in any event, there is likely to be some opportunity for movement in the stock when the initial price is low.

In the figure of the Duke of Plaza-Toro in *The Gondoliers* (1889) Gilbert introduced a man who more than compensated for his doubtful military talents with a real appreciation of the opportunities afforded by modern business. The duke and his worthy spouse found considerable profit in selling their aristocratic endorsements of worthless products and securities. As the duke puts it:

> Those pressing prevailers,
> The ready-made tailors,
>> Quote me as their great double-barrel—
>
> I allow them to do so,
> Though Robinson Crusoe
>> Would jib at their wearing apparel—
>
> I sit, by selection,
> Upon the direction
>> Of several Companies bubble—
>
> As soon as they're floated,
> I'm freely bank-noted—
>> I'm pretty well paid for my trouble.

Both sources of endorsement income which were available to the duke remain open to the notables of our day although subjected to increasing scrutiny by the public. The duke did well by endorsing products which he did not use and business ventures to which he lent only his name. In 1971 the Federal Trade Commission had occasion to question whether veterans of the Indianapolis 500 had sufficient expertise in toy cars to justify their endorsements for the Mattel Company. Government inquiries have also considered whether certain franchise systems that invoke the names of heroes of the sports world are actually engaging the time and energies of the great men.

But the Duke of Plaza-Toro is not only aware of the profit to be drawn from business endorsements; he is also the first Gilbert character to evince knowledge of the advantages of incorporation under the Companies Act of 1862. That statute, on which Gilbert was to lavish his satirical attentions, is often regarded as the source of modern English corporation law and has been referred to as the "magna carta of co-operative enterprise." Actually the act was not an innovative piece of legislation but merely the recodification of a number of earlier nineteenth-century statutory developments. The history of modern company law, to use the British terminology, began in 1825 with the repeal of the Bubble Act. The Bubble Act had been passed in 1720 in reaction to a series of fraudulent securities offerings of which the so-called "South Sea Bubble" was the most famous. Until its repeal in 1825, the Bubble Act generally prohibited the use of corporations unless the corporation was specially authorized by act of Parliament or royal charter. By a series of separate acts beginning with 1825, the availability of corporate business forms was gradually expanded, although the privilege of limited liability which is the hallmark of the modern corporation was introduced only by the Joint Stock Companies Act of 1856. The principal function of the Companies Act of 1862 was to consolidate the 1856 Act with five statutes subsequently passed, and to elaborate the provisions dealing with liquidation ("winding up") of corporations.

In *The Gondoliers*, the Duke of Plaza-Toro, although very much a nobleman, is "unhappily in straitened circumstances at present" and sees advantages in incorporation. Feeling that his social influence is much more extensive than his personal resources, he has permitted a syndicate to organize a corporation to exploit him. The company is to be called the Duke of Plaza-Toro, Limited. An influential directorate has been secured by the syndicate, and the duke himself is to join the board after the original shares have been allotted.

Somehow, Gilbert always seemed to associate the prospect of formation of a corporation with the ultimate possibility of liquidation without full satisfaction of creditors. The duke's daughter, who has been pronounced Queen of Barataria, expresses concern that she "may be called upon at any time to witness her honoured sire in process of liquidation." The duchess is compelled to acknowledge that possibility, but turns aside her daughter's worry with a typical Gilbertian pun: "If your father should stop, it will, of course be necessary to wind him up." Happily *The Gondoliers* comes to a conclusion before the duke's company has an opportunity to fall upon evil days. In fact, we learn in act 2 that, although the duke personally is ninety-five quarters in arrear, he has just been floated at a premium and registered under the Limited Liability Act. We must, however, remain in doubt as to whether the success of the offering would have changed the first reaction of the duke's daughter that there was something "degrading" in the concept of "a Grandee of Spain turned into a public company."

In *Utopia, Limited*, written four years later, the comic prospect was to broaden into the panorama of an entire society transforming itself into a public corporation under the Companies Act of 1862. The opera tells of a tropical island country, Utopia, which has had great difficulty choosing an appropriate form of government. After unsuccessful experiments in democracy, it has hit upon a dangerous variant of the notion of constitutional monarchy. The king of Utopia is trailed around by a bomb-laden official, named the Public Exploder, who is authorized to blow the king up upon "his very first lapse from political or social propriety." The governmental form thus evolved is described by a courtier as "a Despotism tempered by Dynamite." (One wonders, in view of the irruption of violence into American political processes, whether our country is not becoming a Republic tempered by Revolvers.)

An opportunity for a further reform of Utopian society is provided by the return of its Princess Zara from England, where she has taken a high academic degree. She brings home with her a delegation consisting of

Gilbert reading *Utopia, Limited* to the cast at the Savoy Theatre. To Gilbert's right are Sullivan and D'Oyly Carte.

representatives of the main bulwarks of British society whose mission is to remake Utopia in the image of Great Britain. The delegation, named the "Flowers of Progress," consists of a British lord chamberlain, officers of the army and navy (including our old friend, Captain Corcoran from the good ship Pinafore), a queen's counsel and member of Parliament who represents both law and national government, and a spokesman for the new county council system that had just been introduced in England. A leading member of the delegation is Mr. Goldbury, a company promoter. He produces the central idea for the restructuring of Utopia—instead of remaining a monarchy, it should register as a corporation under the Companies Act of 1862. In support of his proposal, he launches into a song of praise of the corporate form, a song which among its other virtues contains one of the finest working definitions of corporate capital, at least from the point of view of creditors. Capital, according to Mr. Goldbury, is "a public declaration to what extent they mean to pay their debts." Since Mr. Goldbury's song is a great comic tribute to the corporation and also an important key to Gilbert's corporate satire, it deserves to be set down at length:

> Some seven men form an Association
>   (If possible, all Peers and Baronets),
> They start off with a public declaration
>   To what extent they mean to pay their debts.
> That's called their Capital: if they are wary
>   They will not quote it at a sum immense.
> The figure's immaterial—it may vary
>   From eighteen million down to eighteenpence.
>   *I* should put it rather low;
>   The good sense of doing so
>   Will be evident at once to any debtor.
>   When it's left to you to say
>   What amount you mean to pay,
>   Why, the lower you can put it at, the better.
>
> They then proceed to trade with all who'll trust 'em,
>   Quite irrespective of their capital
> (It's shady, but it's sanctified by custom);
>   Bank, Railway, Loan, or Panama Canal.
> You can't embark on trading too tremendous—
>   It's strictly fair, and based on common sense—
> If you succeed, your profits are stupendous—
>   And if you fail, pop goes your eighteenpence.
>   Make the money-spinner spin!
>   For you only stand to win,
>   And you'll never with dishonesty be twitted,
>   For nobody can know,
>   To a million or so,
>   To what extent your capital's committed!

> If you come to grief, and creditors are craving
>   (For nothing that is planned by mortal head
> Is certain in this Vale of Sorrow—saving
>   That one's Liability is Limited),—
> Do you suppose that signifies perdition?
>   If so you're but a monetary dunce—
> You merely file a Winding-Up Petition,
>   And start another Company at once!
>   Though a Rothschild you may be
>   In your own capacity,
> As a Company you've come to utter sorrow—
>   But the Liquidators say,
>   'Never mind—you needn't pay,'
> So you start another Company to-morrow!

The gospel of the corporation, as recited by Goldbury, at first sight strikes the king of Utopia as dishonest but he concludes that if it's good enough for virtuous England, it's good enough for his own backward island. The royal court, given the green light by its monarch's approval, takes up Goldbury's project with enthusiasm and, in fact, act 1 of *Utopia, Limited* concludes with what may be the only choral tribute to a corporation statute in all the pages of opera:

> All hail, astonishing Fact!
> All hail, Invention new—
> The Joint Stock Company's Act—
> The Act of Sixty-Two!

The second act shows the far-reaching effects of incorporation on Utopia's economy and political life. Mr. Goldbury, flushed with his success at turning the monarchy into a corporation, carries the reorganization to its logical conclusion. Discarding the theory of the 1862 Act that there is magic in the number seven (the number of individual incorporators required under the Act for formation of a corporation), Goldbury has constituted every man, woman and child in Utopia a limited liability company with liability restricted to the amount of his declared capital. Princess Zara asserts that "there is not a christened baby in Utopia who has not already issued his little Prospectus." The princess's favorite Flower of Progress, Captain Fitzbattleaxe, marvels at the power of a civilization to transmute, by the magic word of incorporation, "a Limited Income into an Income Limited."

Universal incorporation, as Gilbert portrays it, proves more attractive to the promoters than to the corporations' creditors. Scaphio, a judge of Utopia's Supreme Court, has been moonlighting as an apparel supplier. He contracts to supply the entire nation with a complete set of

English clothes (so that they may be Anglicized externally as well as within). When he sends his bills, the customers plead liability limited to a declared capital of eighteenpence and apply to have the debt discharged by corporate liquidation under the winding-up provisions of the Companies Act. In Gilbert's "corporate state," the king has no jurisdiction over grievances such as Scaphio's, but must request him to lay his complaint before the next Board meeting of Utopia, Limited.

The device of incorporation also profoundly affects the relations of the king with courtiers (including the disappointed Scaphio) who plot his death. Since the king is no longer a human being but a company, they can no longer blow him up; at best they can only seek to "wind him up" by corporate liquidation proceedings, a small source of emotional satisfaction for the king's violent foes.

Towards the end of the opera, the Flowers of Progress, by their Anglicizing programs including universal incorporation, have achieved such a stable society that they alienate those who thrive on disorder. The opponents of "progress" then decide to overthrow the works of the reformers by introducing the one overlooked force in English government which will assure permanent chaos—party government. With the introduction of party government the regime of Monarchy, Limited is transformed in a wink into a Limited Monarchy.

Even this brief overview of *Utopia* should provide convincing proof that Darlington is wrong in supposing Gilbert to be ignorant of the nature of corporations. It is of interest, however, to consider why Gilbert found corporations to be a worthy object of satire.

There is no doubt that the "magic" of incorporation particularly appealed to Gilbert's penchant for fantasy. Just as he could never get over the belief that a magic love potion transforming a stern clergyman into an impetuous lover was the most humorous of plot devices, so he found worthy of laughter the legal device that permitted the transformation of individual businessmen into a corporate entity. How he would have roared with laughter had he learned with us that Howard Hughes by a legal assignment to the Rosemont Corporation reciting $10 consideration could literally transform his life and all biographical rights into a corporate asset!

But if we pause to focus on Gilbert's view of the corporate idea as a false denial of the uncertainties of human life, we will have come to an understanding of a deeper layer of his criticism of the corporation. Gilbert's most personal view of life, at least as he grew older, appears to have been strongly pessimistic. The king of Utopia summarizes the human condition in as dark a color as the final chorus from Verdi's *Falstaff*. The king laments:

> Ill you've thriven—
> Ne'er in clover;
> Lastly, when
> Three-score and ten
> (And not till then)
> The joke is over!

To Gilbert the corporation and the doctrine of limited liability are symbols of artificial endeavors to insulate the individual from the ever-present possibility of disaster in his affairs. As Mr. Goldbury comments in his song of corporations:

> For nothing that is planned by mortal head
> Is certain in this Vale of Sorrow—saving
> That one's Liability is Limited.

More narrowly, the corporate idea to Gilbert was faulty in that it shielded the incompetent and the irresponsible man from the consequences of his own failure. It is for this reason that Gilbert leapt with special delight on the provisions for discharge of corporate obligations through the liquidation or winding-up provisions of the Companies Act of 1862. We can be reasonably sure that he was thinking in this connection not only of the business world at large but also of his own world of the theatre. In his short play, *Actors, Authors, and Audiences*, he deals with failure of a theatre manager in much the same manner as he attacks corporate liquidation in *Utopia*: "[Theatre management] is a very easy profession to master. If you make a success, you pocket the profits; if you fail, you close your theatre abruptly, and a benefit performance is organized on your behalf. Then you begin again." Compare the words of Mr. Goldbury in *Utopia* on the delights of corporate winding-up:

> As a Company you've come to utter sorrow—
> But the Liquidators say,
> 'Never mind—you needn't pay,'
> So you start another Company to-morrow!

Perhaps Gilbert's identification of corporate problems with theatre management had been strengthened by the fact that *Utopia* was written shortly after his famous quarrels with his partners, Sullivan and D'Oyly Carte, over the administration of the Savoy Theatre. The identification of corporation and theatre survived in the last Gilbert and Sullivan opera, *The Grand Duke* (1896). In *The Grand Duke*, Gilbert unsuccessfully mimicked *Utopia* by describing a conspiracy by a group of actors to overthrow a dukedom and remodel it along the lines of a theatrical company.

The most interesting element of Gilbert's criticism of the corporation, however, lies in his suggestion that the privileges of incorporation, public corporate financing, and limited liability are undeserved unless accompanied by high standards of responsibility by corporate management. The corporate form, for the promoter Goldbury, is a device for raising funds from the public for doubtful schemes, and with minimal risk of accountability. To the populace of Utopia it becomes a means of buying goods for which it has neither the means nor the intention to pay.

The force of Gilbert's attack on corporate morality appears to have been lost on even perceptive observers. George Bernard Shaw, reviewing *Utopia* as a music critic for London's *Saturday Review*, wrote that he "enjoyed the score of Utopia more than that of any previous Savoy operas," and that "the book has Mr. Gilbert's lighter qualities without his faults." However, he scantly summarized Gilbert's "main idea" as "the Anglicization of Utopia by a people boundlessly credulous as to the superiority of the English race" and made no reference to the satire of principles of corporate law and practice. *Punch*, unlike Shaw, was extremely critical of *Utopia*. Its 1893 review of the new offering of the team that *Punch* was addicted to calling Gillivan and Sulbert (in tribute, one would hope, to the uncanny blending of their gifts) made no substantial comment on the book except to accuse Gilbert of plagiarizing a scene presenting a court reception in the semicircular stage arrangement popularized by the Christy Minstrels.

Even with the advantage of historical retrospection, twentieth-century critics often apparently fail to see that the corporate law satire was firmly rooted in the business scandals in Gilbert's times. Thus W. A. Darlington writes of *Utopia*: "It would be interesting to know just why Gilbert fell foul of the Joint Stock Company Act of 1862 at this particular period in his life, more than a quarter of a century after the act had become law." Clues to the answer to Darlington's question are provided for all to see in Mr. Goldbury's song. Mr. Goldbury sings of the management of the spanking-new, thinly incorporated firm:

> They then proceed to trade with all who'll trust 'em,
> Quite irrespective of their capital
> (It's shady, but it's sanctified by custom);
> Bank, Railway, Loan, or Panama Canal.

These lines reveal that Gilbert was not merely attacking the concept of limited liability as an abstraction, but that he was well aware of frauds that had been perpetrated on the public by unprincipled men using the advantages of corporate form.

The reference to banks in Mr. Goldbury's song might have awakened memories of a number of bank failures in England in the latter part of the nineteenth century, but it is likely that Gilbert intended to allude to the Glasgow Bank fraud case of 1878. The closing of the City of Glasgow Bank in October 1878 led to criminal proceedings resulting in the conviction of five directors and the bank manager on charges relating to the falsification of balance sheets. It was charged that the directors had produced false balance sheets and declared large dividends in order to cover up the insolvency of the bank. The bank's downfall had been contributed to by improvident loans including substantial loans to the defendant directors and their firms.

The City of Glasgow Bank had lost no time in incorporating under the Joint Stock Company Act of 1862 in the very year of its adoption and Gilbert may be forgiven for doubting whether the insiders had in their stewardship justified the protection given to them by the new legislation. Major Arthur Griffiths's account, in his *Mysteries of Police and Crime* (1899), of the behavior of one of the directors prior to the bank's closing could hardly have been bettered by Gilbert's own pen:

> One shareholder in September, a month before the failure, called at the office of Mr. Stewart, saying he had heard unpleasant rumours about the bank. Mr. Stewart, a director, who . . . was largely in debt to the bank, answered that there were always rumours current about everybody. Then Mr. Stewart went out and did not return, being clearly anxious to cut short an inconvenient interview.

The most recent business scandal referred to in the quoted lines of Mr. Goldbury's song was the welter of criminal charges growing out of the failure of the Panama Canal construction program by the French-controlled Panama Company. In February of 1893, eight months prior to the opening of *Utopia*, the aged Ferdinand de Lesseps, hero of the building of the Suez Canal, his son, and two others were found guilty of fraud in an 1888 bond issue to raise funds for the canal project, of attempted fraud in another aborted bond issue, and of misappropriation of company funds. The fraud charges, expressed in the elegant language of French statute as the use of fraudulent means to raise hopes for the realization of a chimerical event, rested on misrepresentations made by the defendants with respect to the cost and likely completion date of the canal and levels of expected revenues. Although the conviction was upset on appeal (on the basis of the statute of limitations) before *Utopia* opened, the facts of the case lingered.

In March of the same year, five French legislators, the former public works minister and his private secretary, and the younger de Lesseps, faced a bribery trial in which it was charged that the public officials had been bribed by the Panama Company in an effort to secure favorable legislation and governmental action in connection with the Company's financing plans. The legislators were acquitted but the other defendants were found guilty.

The allegations of misconduct, which were the subject of these trials, only singled out from a bizarre pattern of financial behavior those acts with which the criminal law of the time could most easily come to grips. Very little of the procedure used in the Panama Canal financings bears any resemblance to what might be considered permissible under the regulatory system of our own Securities and Exchange Commission. In addition to the alleged attempts on the integrity of the French government, the administrators of the Canal Company made widespread use of company funds to pay newspapers for publishing favorable stories on the progress of the Canal. Far from considering such payments to reflect doubtful business morality, the Canal Company reported such payments in its financial statements under the wonderfully euphemistic account heading "publicité." Apparently, the newspapermen were even less shy about the payments than the Company and considered the amount of the payoffs to afford a measure of the value of their editorial pages. Maron J. Simon reports in his study of the Canal scandals that one editor sued the auditor for the liquidated company for understating the amounts which the Panama Company had paid his newspaper.

The events in France were not lost on Gilbert or on the English public. The *London Times* carried detailed stories on the Panama enterprise and the litigation which resulted. Moreover, by the spring of 1893 much of the passion and curiosity aroused by the Panama affair had focused on the figure of a "mystery man" then residing in England— Cornelius Herz, an international charlatan, confidence man, and friend of influential men in political and financial circles. Herz, who had been accused of complicity in the Panama scandal, was during the whole of 1893 and for many years thereafter holed up in the Tankerville Hotel in Bournemouth, England, where he waged a successful battle against extradition to France on the basis of his medical condition. The French legislators, in their eagerness to talk to Herz, resolved that if illness would not permit him to come to them, they would question him at his bedside. However, the interview, which was scheduled for July 1897, never came off. Herz reneged at the last minute and this disappointing news was transmitted to the group of twenty-five deputies who were to visit him just as they were about to board the channel steamer.

Although the Panama Canal case continued to make history for many years, by 1893 it had already been assured a measure of immortality in the words and music of *Utopia, Limited*. It was an affair which supplied all the major elements of Gilbert's satirical view of corporate finance—the famous man whose name inspired investors' confidence (de Lesseps); a securities offering based on unjustified claims of bonanza; the "free bank-noting" of newspapers and others whose sponsorship of the offering was desired; and finally the liquidation of failed corporate enterprise.

Despite his jokes at the expense of the corporation and limited liability, and his likely disillusionment with the business practices of his own time, Gilbert shows such balanced judgment in his works that we cannot assume he was proposing an outright repeal of the Companies Act. Indeed, if he attacked limited liability in *Utopia*, we must recall that in the earlier *Pirates of Penzance* (1879), he had assaulted with equal force the notion of *unlimited* individual liability, the observance of contract unmodified by protective considerations of public policy. In that opera the young hero Frederic is mocked by Gilbert as a "slave of duty" because he undertakes literal and strict performance of his pirate apprenticeship until his twenty-first birthday as provided by his indenture, even though the term of performance will last eighty-four years since his birthday falls on February 29 in leap year.

In fact, I am not sure that Gilbert's critique of the corporation is inapposite to the debate that continues in modern governmental and academic circles as to the proper scope of corporate responsibilities. In return for the protections and privileges of corporate form and the opportunities of large business corporations to amass wealth and power, the expectations for social contribution by corporations have greatly increased. Discussions that decades ago turned on obligations of corporations for charitable gifts and local community activity have broadened to include demands relating to basic business policy, such as ecological and safety concerns, minority group hiring, and corporate attitudes towards war and colonialism. Nobody would hazard a guess where Gilbert would have stood on the myriad of public issues faced by the modern corporation, but I think he would have been at home with the notion that the responsibility of a corporation may be far broader than its legal liability.

It is difficult to come away from a study of *Utopia, Limited* and of Gilbert's other literary expressions of interest in law without feeling that his work has suffered the double injustice of having been denied "relevancy" either to the problems of posterity or to the important issues of his own day. How much better we would do were we to read his librettos in the spirit of the counsel given by the jester, Jack Point, in *The Yeomen of the Guard*:

> Oh, winnow all my folly, and you'll find
> A grain or two of truth among the chaff!

The Unpleasantness at the Garrick Club

The controversy at London's Garrick Club over the expulsion of member Edmund Yates in 1858 led to the rupture of the fragile friendship of Dickens and Thackeray. Since the Garrick Club was organized by patrons of the theatre, it is fitting that the Club's *cause célèbre* assumed the features of tragicomedy, and it is in that form that it will be presented here.

The Setting: The Garrick Club, Covent Garden, 1858

The Garrick Club (named for the great actor David Garrick) was founded in 1831 at No. 35 King Street, near the northwest corner of the Covent Garden Market. The purposes and membership of the Club were later described in a Club report:

> [It was founded] for the purpose of bringing together the patrons of the drama and its professors, and also for offering literary men a rendezvous. . . . Nearly all the leading actors are members, and there are few of the active literary men of the day who are not upon the list. The large majority is composed of representatives of all the best classes.

Despite the snobbish tone of this announcement, the Club's purpose to allow actors to mingle with their aristocratic admirers on equal terms was truly revolutionary in view of the fact that "theatricals" had generally been denied admission to respectable social establishments. In the very year of the formation of the Garrick Club, actors were excluded

The Dining Hall of the Garrick Club.

from London's "Beefsteak Society," although the door was open to lawyers, authors, painters and even theatre managers—so long as they resisted the temptation to appear on stage. The Garrick provided actors a noble home, under the titular presidency of the Duke of Devonshire. The roster of charter members included the famous actors William Macready, Charles Kemble, and Tyrone Power, as well as the architect Sir John Soane, and the author of *The Ingoldsby Legends*, Canon Richard Harris Barham, who served as Club rhymer.

In view of the association of the Club with the theatre, its location in the heart of London's theatre district was appropriate. Thackeray has left us a beautiful picture of the Garden as it existed at the time of his Garrick membership—a description now doubly poignant because of the ravages which modern city planning has wrought:

> The two great national theatres on one side, a churchyard full of mouldy but undying celebrities on the other; a fringe of houses studded in every part with anecdote and history; an arcade, often more gloomy and deserted than a cathedral aisle; a rich cluster of brown old taverns—one of them filled with the counterfeit presentment of many actors long since silent, who scowl or smile once more from the canvas upon the grandsons of their dead admirers; a something in the air which breathes of old books, old pictures, old painters, and old authors; a place beyond all other places one would choose in which to hear the chimes at midnight; . . .

Dramatis Personae and Prologue: Dickens, Thackeray, and Yates

Dickens and Thackeray had known each other since 1836. Their first encounter was distinctly disappointing from Thackeray's point of view. Thackeray, who was a clever caricaturist, submitted some proposed sketches for *Pickwick Papers*, but Dickens rejected them. "Strange to say," Thackeray recalled in a speech in 1858 (the year of the Garrick Club affair), "[Dickens] did not find [the sketches] suitable." Over the years the two men appeared to establish a friendly personal relationship, although the degree of their congeniality remains a matter of varying interpretation. They exchanged household visits and we read of one Christmas party which Thackeray and his children attended at Dickens's Tavistock House. At the end of this party Young Charley, at his father's instruction, led the Dickens children in a chorus of cheers for the departing Thackeray. Thackeray was also invited to a performance of *Tom Thumb* by the Dickens family. The two authors appeared at public dinners together and Dickens chaired a farewell dinner for Thackeray prior to his second American tour. On another occasion Thackeray smoked a cigar with Dickens before leaving on a walking tour of Scotland. The Dickens and Thackeray families appeared to become closer after they found themselves near neighbors in Boulogne in 1854. Katey and Mary Dickens became fast friends of the two Thackeray girls, and Thackeray commented that he was always inclined to think well of "anybody who is kind to my women."

However, there were many sources of incompatibility between Dickens and Thackeray, public, literary, and personal, which posed continuing threats to their friendship. Although their shared disgust with the conduct of the Crimean War brought them into brief political alliance in the service of the Administrative Reform Society, their general social views were divergent. Thackeray was not, like Dickens, dedicated to basic reform. It may have been of himself he spoke when he gave the words to Henry Esmond: "I can't but accept the world as I find it, including a rope's end, as long as it is in fashion." Dickens's attacks on the materialistic roots of Victorian society reflected a degree of rebelliousness Thackeray could not share, although many of Dickens's insights into contemporary social phenomena appear akin to his own. When Thackeray fought successfully against Douglas Jerrold's brand of radical journalism in *Punch* in the 1840s, he found that Dickens rallied to the aid of his adversary. Many years later, they again found themselves in controversy over what Dickens judged to be Thackeray's overly sentimental praise of the work of the Charterhouse Charity.

In the course of their careers, Thackeray and Dickens also took opposite positions in many controversies affecting the literary profession. When Thackeray fell out with their mutual friend John Forster in 1847, Dickens supported Forster but was able to arrange a reconciliation dinner without impairing his own friendship with Thackeray. The two men also skirmished over the status of the literary profession and its rights to public financial support. Dickens was a strong defender of the dignity of the profession and advocated the grant of pensions to authors. Thackeray, as secure in his Anglo-Indian birth as in his sense of his literary talent, argued that the able writer needed no special protection. He irritated his fellow writers by lampooning the disorder of journalists' lives in *Pendennis* and burlesquing the styles of some of his contemporaries in *Punch*. Dickens appears to have awaited with trepidation a parody of his own writing. In fact, Thackeray intended the series to end with burlesques of Dickens—and the final turn of the screw—of Thackeray himself, but the *Punch* proprietors vetoed the idea. It is generally accepted that Dickens's concept of Thackeray's alternately cynical and enthusiastic attitudes towards life and art is incorporated in the portrait of the fake-Bohemian Henry Gowan in *Little Dorrit*. Thackeray may not have recognized the resemblance, but he is known to have remarked that "Little D. is damned stupid."

The responses of Dickens and Thackeray to each other's books were quite different. With the exception of *Denis Duval* (which appeared after Thackeray's death), Dickens only praised one of Thackeray's works warmly, *The Curate's Walk*, a minor sentimental London sketch. Even in the letter to Thackeray in which he recorded the tears he shed over *The Curate's Walk*, Dickens reveals how he held back from exploration of major Thackeray works: "I have nothing more to confess but that I am saving up the perusal of Vanity Fair until I shall have done Dombey."

Thackeray, on the other hand, was a great and generous admirer of Dickens's works and praised them enthusiastically, not only in public lectures but also (where praise really counts) in private correspondence and conversation. Not all of Dickens's books pleased Thackeray equally. If he rated *Pickwick* below the work of Fielding, we must remember Thackeray's rejected illustrations. Thackeray also attacked *Oliver Twist* as falsely glamorizing crime and low life. But of *A Christmas Carol* he said: "It seems to me a national benefit, and to every man or woman who reads it a personal kindness." In separate letters to his friends the Brookfields he urged them to read *David Copperfield*, in which he found "those inimitable Dickens touches which make such a great man of him." However, this praise was mixed with a sense of rivalry and inferiority. He added in his letter to Rev. Brookfield that *David Copperfield* beat the current number of *Pendennis* hollow but commented to Mrs. Brookfield that *Copperfield*'s simplified style showed the influence of *Vanity Fair*. And even his masterpiece *Vanity Fair* seemed to him less powerful than *Dombey*. He exclaimed to Mark Lemon, the *Punch* editor, pounding on his table for emphasis, "There's no writing against such power as this—One has no chance! Read that chapter describing young Paul's death; it is unsurpassed—it is stupendous!" Thackeray's love for Dickens's books was shared by his daughters. In manuscript reminiscences he wrote that his daughter Minnie named her cats after Dickens characters, and in a public lecture in New York he reported his rueful answer to her question as to why he did not write books like Mr. Dickens: "Who can?"

After the appearance of *Vanity Fair* Thackeray's feeling of rivalry with Dickens sharpened. "Dickens mistrusts me," he had already written ten years earlier, and now he commented: "I am become a sort of great man in my way—all but at the top of the tree; indeed there if the truth were known and having a great fight up there with Dickens." The literary adherents of the two men took every opportunity to push their chieftains into opposition.

In addition to professional rivalry, the difference in the family origins of the two men may also have played an inhibiting role in their relations. Dickens, a grandson of houseservants and grandson and namesake of an escaped embezzler, was haunted by a fear of the snobbery of others while Thackeray was a self-confessed snob. In 1849 Thackeray wrote to Mrs. Brookfield, "I met on the pier . . . the great Dickens with his wife his children his Miss Hogarth all looking abominably coarse vulgar and happy. . . ."

One of the social settings of the friendship of Dickens and Thackeray was the Garrick Club, which Thackeray entered in 1833 and Dickens first joined in 1837 during the triumphant appearance of the *Pickwick* installments. By the 1850s the Garrick Club seems to have been split into two factions, the older members with whom Thackeray was on cordial terms (and over whom, according to one memoirist, he reigned as "a sort of Dictator"), and a more Bohemian element which tended to look to Dickens as one of its leaders. Despite the attachment of this latter group to Dickens, it is apparent that the Garrick Club was of only peripheral interest to him. Although he loved the theatre and was an amateur actor, he seldom came to the Club and his membership history was quite spotty. We sometimes hear of people who join organizations in the hope that some day they will have an opportunity to resign in righteous indignation. Whether that was the case with Dickens, we do not know. However, the record shows that he resigned from the Club in November of 1838, the year after his admission. He joined again six years later in January, 1844 and withdrew in June, 1856, rejoining once more on November of the same year.

Thackeray, on the other hand, was an ardent clubman. This was only a natural development since his home life was tragically destroyed early in his marriage by the hopeless mental illness of his wife, who was committed to an institution in the winter of 1841–42. Although Thackeray was touchingly devoted to his two daughters, Annie and Minnie, his great gregariousness caused him to find a substitute for the domestic hearth in the clubs of London. The Garrick Club, famed for the high spirits and wit of its members, was his favorite. In a speech at the Club in its early days, Thackeray said, "Do we, its happy inmates, ever speak of it as 'The Garrick Club'? No, but as 'The G.,' the little 'G.,' the dearest place in the world." Percy Fitzgerald, a historian of the Club and a friend of Dickens and Forster, writes that Thackeray "was during his time the Club itself—its centre, its soul, its cynosure. It was his very home, not a mere 'house of call' . . . It seemed to be a sort of whetting-stone for his wit; it kept his humours bright, keen and polished."

In view of Thackeray's attachment to the Garrick and to London club life, it is not surprising that we find in his writings many descriptions of London clubs and their oddly-assorted members. In his *Book of Snobs* (to whose title Thackeray added a characteristically insightful tag "By One of Themselves") he devoted several chapters to a discussion of Club Snobs. Two of the Club Snobs, Colonel Bludyer and Ranville Ranville, look askance at the admission of literary men into their Club. Bludyer, glaring at "the present Snob" (Thackeray), warns: "Infernal impudent jackanapes! If he shows me up, I'll break every bone in his skin." Ranville comments: "These people are very well in their proper places, and as a public man, I make a point of shaking hands with them, and that sort of thing; but to have one's privacy obtruded upon by such people is really too much."

In a chapter of *Mr. Brown's Letters To His Nephew*, Thackeray's series of London sketches, Mr. Brown the Elder introduces Mr. Brown the Younger into a club, the Polyanthus, into which young Pen is also admitted in *Pendennis*. One would hope that the Polyanthus did not resemble the Garrick, since its members' activities are limited to smoking, billiards, cards, hogging the daily newspapers, and tyrannizing the poorer members. Thackeray also wrote a short sketch in which the immediate impact of the French Revolution of 1848 on the English public is measured by the rumors exchanged at a London club, and in a chapter of a travel book he reports clubhouse gossip in Gibraltar. One of Thackeray's last sketches, "Strange To Say, On Club Paper," reports clubmembers' baseless slanders on a deceased member who was reported to have drawn up a codicil at his country home, on Athenaeum Club stationery. If a man could take Club stationery for personal use miles away, they murmured, how could the spoons be safe? But these pieces are minor Thackeray. English literature is in his debt for his humorous love and observation of club life as they are reflected in the famous opening scene of *Pendennis*. In the following passage Thackeray describes the quiet mastery with which Major Pendennis made a favorite Club table his own:

> He always took possession of the same table in the same corner of the room, from which nobody ever thought of ousting him. One or two mad wags and wild fellows had, in former days, endeavoured to deprive him of this place; but there was a quiet dignity in the Major's manner as he took his seat at the next table, and surveyed the interlopers, which rendered it impossible for any man to sit and breakfast under his eye; and that table—by the fire, and yet near the window—became his own.

Of course, it would be foolish to assert, without preparing to face the just wrath of the spirit of Mr. Pickwick, that there are no clubs in Dickens. But they are not the great London clubs, but small, idiosyncratic groups founded by dominant figures. Besides Mr. Pickwick's scholarly company we have Master Humphrey's Clock and its below-stairs spinoff, Mr. Weller's Watch, as well as the Eight Club described in an unpublished fragment of *The Mystery of Edwin Drood*. It can be said accurately that in the imaginative world of his fiction Dickens did not join clubs—he created his own (just as he did during his stay on the Isle of Wight in the summer of 1849, when he formed a club called the "Sea Serpents," which spent pleasant evenings drinking, playing games, and applauding his conjuring tricks). I do not think it is accidental that Dickens did not write of the London clubs. They did not mean as much to him as they did to Thackeray, and there lay the seed of the unhappy confrontation that was to follow.

The tenure of Edmund Yates at the Garrick, which ended in uproar, began in subterfuge. Having the appearance of a full-grown man while still adolescent, he entered the Club at seventeen, under the age prescribed by the regulations. His father, the actor Frederick Yates, was an original member of the Club. The elder Yates performed as Mantalini, Quilp, and Fagin in successful adaptations of *Nicholas Nickleby, The Old Curiosity Shop*, and *Oliver Twist*, and Dickens praised him highly. Frederick's talent, and the celebrated beauty of Mrs. Yates, a gifted actress whom Dickens also admired, predisposed Dickens favorably towards the young Yates. Edmund early embarked on a career of gossipy journalism and his column, "A Lounger At The Clubs," advertised that he intended to use club rooms as a principal source of his tittle-tattle.

Yates was a devoted follower of Dickens and a reliable ally in his personal and literary conflicts. However, in his memoirs Yates also expressed great admiration for Thackeray and attributed his choice of a career in journalism to his reading of *Pendennis*.

Act One: Epsom and the Garrick Club

The year 1858 was a difficult one for Dickens, and the personal strain under which he labored may have obscured his judgment in assessing Thackeray's sensitivities in the controversy that was to arise at the Garrick. Dickens had carried out his painful decision to separate from his wife and was upset by many wild rumors linking his name with Ellen Ternan and his sister-in-law Georgina Hogarth. Bound as intimately as any author has ever been to the hearts and judgments of his audience, Dickens felt a compulsion to put before the public his denial of these slanders, which he attributed to the hostility of his mother-in-law and his sister-in-law Helen. Friends and publishers who opposed his wishes to publish his apologia felt the full weight of his frustration and anger. Dickens never forgave Mark Lemon for his refusal to insert his personal statement in *Punch*, although Lemon may have believed with justification that the statement did not meet the magazine's standards of humor. Dickens extended his resentment to Bradbury & Evans, publisher of *Punch* and of Dickens's books, and ultimately severed all business relations with the firm, returning to his former publisher, Chapman & Hall.

While this storm was gathering, Thackeray added new ground for Dickens's irritation. On May 14 while visiting the Derby race at Epsom,

Thackeray first learned from an acquaintance rumors that were circulating regarding Dickens's involvement with Ellen Ternan. A few days later at the Garrick, Thackeray was told of Dickens's impending separation. When it was suggested to him that Dickens was leaving his wife "on account of an intrigue with his sister-in-law" Georgina, Thackeray drew on the Epsom rumors and came to the clumsy defense of his friend: "no says I no such thing—its with an actress."

For an equally maladroit defense against rumor one would have to go back to the days of the Roman epigrammist Martial, who wrote: "He who fancies that Acerra reeks of yesterday's wine is wrong. Acerra always drinks till daylight." Dickens's campfollowers, who lost no opportunity to exacerbate his suspicion of his rival, reported Thackeray's blunder to him as evidence of malice. "We shall never be allowed to be friends that's clear," Thackeray wrote to his mother.

Act Two, Scene One: A Printer's Office

The controversy at the Garrick was actually due to the need for newspaper column filler—a need which, fortunately, is customarily supplied by "many cheerful facts" about the height of Mount Everest. Edmund Yates, in the third week of his employment with the little periodical *Town Talk*, went to the printer's office. There he heard to his horror that because of illness, Watts Phillips, a cartoonist and political contributor, had not sent in his usual quota and that another column of original material was necessary. "There was no help for it," Yates later recalled, "I took off my coat—literally, I remember, for it was a warm evening—mounted a high stool at a high desk, and commenced to cudgel my brains." Having had great success with a sketch of Dickens during the previous week's number, Yates made a fatal choice—he would follow up with a similar portrait of Dickens's great rival Thackeray.

The major part of the little article dealt with Thackeray's literary career and mingled praise with criticism. Yates extolled *Vanity Fair*: "This great work . . . with perhaps the exception of *The Newcomes*, is the most perfect literary dissection of the human heart." However, Yates noted a falling off of Thackeray's later work in popularity and interest. He went on to criticize Thackeray for trimming to the taste of his audience by flattering the aristocracy in England, while worshipping George Washington and attacking the "Four Georges" while in America. Yates also asserted that there was a "want of heart in all he writes."

Had Yates limited himself to literary criticism, the Garrick Club might have remained at peace. But unaccountably he chose to begin his

Edmund Yates.

column with an unflattering description of Thackeray's appearance and an even less favorable appraisal of his personality:

> His face is bloodless, and not particularly expressive, but remarkable for the fracture of the bridge of the nose, the result of an accident in youth. . . . No one meeting him could fail to recognise in him a gentleman; his bearing is cold and uninviting, his style of conversation either openly cynical or affectedly good-natured and benevolent; his *bonhomie* is forced, his wit biting, his pride easily touched. . . .

The literary reservations of such an unimportant young journalist Thackeray would probably have ignored. But the personal attack stung him to the quick. Later, in his essay "On Screens In Dining-Rooms" (1860) in which he responded to an article submitted by Yates to *The*

William Makepeace Thackeray.

New York Times concerning the prospects of *The Cornhill Magazine*, Thackeray stated his feelings about journalists whose stock-in-trade is not literary criticism but the personal conversations of writers:

> Attack our books, Mr. Correspondent, and welcome. They are fair subjects for just censure or praise. . . . But Mr. Nameless, behind the publisher's screen uninvited, peering at the company and the meal, catching up scraps of the jokes, and noting down the guests' behaviour, and conversation—what a figure he is! *Allons*, Mr. Nameless! Put up your notebook; walk out of the hall; and leave gentlemen alone who would be private, and wish you no harm.

The offense in Yates's *Town Talk* column was all the greater since this article appeared to capitalize on private conversations of Thackeray at the Garrick, where he was, in Percy Fitzgerald's words, "cock of the walk." Fitzgerald adds, with more psychological understanding than the literary historians have shown: "To be flouted in this style by 'a stripling' would never do. He would lose all his authority."

And if matters were not bad enough, an unhappy coincidence added an element of possible conspiracy. Yates's article appeared on the very day on which Dickens's defense of his marital conduct appeared in the journal named (quite aptly, in this case) *Household Words*. Thackeray's adherents saw Yates's piece as a flanking attack on Thackeray to neutralize his supposed participation in the gossip about Ellen Ternan.

Act Two, Scene Two: The Garrick Club

Two days after the appearance of his article, Yates received a strongly worded letter from Thackeray asking that in the future Yates "refrain from printing comments upon my private conversations; that you will forego discussions, however blundering, upon my private affairs; and that you will henceforth please to consider any question of my personal truth and sincerity as quite out of the province of your criticism." The heart of Thackeray's attack was his resentment over what he saw as intrusion into the privacy of Club conversations: "We meet at a club, where before you were born, I believe, I and other gentlemen have been in the habit of talking without any idea that our conversation would supply paragraphs for professional vendors of 'Literary Talk;' and I don't remember that out of that club I have ever exchanged six words with you." Thackeray later made similar observations to Charles Kingsley in defense of his response to the Yates article:

> [The Garrick Club] is a social Institution quite unlike other clubs, . . . where men have been in the habit of talking quite freely to one another (in a little room not 15 feet square) for this 1/4 of a century or more. If the penny-a-liner is to come into this sanctum, and publish his comments upon the conversation there held and the people he meets there, it is all over with the comfort and friendliness of our Society.

Despite the merit of Thackeray's invocation of Club privacy, I sometimes wish he had written Yates the pithy response subsequently suggested by Thackeray's staunch friend, Shirley Brooks: "Dear Yates next time you want a guinea write to me not of me."

Yates's immediate reaction to Thackeray's letter was to draft a reply suggesting that Thackeray was an old pot lecturing a young kettle. He listed a number of Thackeray's fellow clubmembers whom Thackeray had attacked in print, including Bulwer-Lytton. Before sending the letter that Yates still felt a quarter-century later would have ended the row, the young man consulted his friend Dickens. If Thackeray erred, as most commentators suggest, by excessive severity to a young journalist, Dickens at this critical juncture appeared to make a mistake equally great. He disapproved Yates's proposed letter, but, instead of attempting to mediate between his two friends, he concurred in Yates's sending a curt rejection of Thackeray's complaint.

Thackeray turned over copies of the exchanged letters to the Committee of the Club and requested a ruling as to whether the practice of publishing articles such as Yates's "will not be fatal to the comfort of the Club, and is not intolerable in a society of gentlemen."

The secretary of the Club notified the antagonists that the Committee would meet on the following Saturday to consider Thackeray's complaint. Yates responded with a letter challenging the Committee's jurisdiction. He observed that "the article makes no reference to the Club, refers to no conversation that took place there." He added that the "article may be in exceedingly bad taste; but . . . the Committee is not a Committee of taste."

The Committee held its meeting and ruled that Yates was to make ample apology to Thackeray or to retire from the Club, and that if Yates declined to do either, a general meeting of the Club would be called to consider the matter. Yates submitted a letter to be read before the general meeting, offering to apologize to the Club but not to Thackeray. Yates stated that he had equal right to an apology from Thackeray, who had in the interim inserted an irrelevant allusion to his foe as "Young Grub-Street" in a current number of *The Virginians.*

On July 10 the general meeting was held; it adopted, by a vote of seventy to forty-eight, a resolution holding Thackeray's complaint well founded and referring the matter to the Committee for appropriate action while at the same time expressing the hope that "a most disagreeable duty may be spared it by Mr. Yates making such ample apology to Mr. Thackeray as may result in the withdrawal of all the unpleasant expressions used in reference to this matter." How one would have loved to be "behind the screen" at the meeting. Yates was supported by speeches by three novelists, Dickens, Wilkie Collins, and Samuel Lover, and by Sir James Ferguson who (according to Yates) hurried home from Palestine to speak and vote in Yates's favor. But the influential Thackeray had the votes.

Act Three, Scene One: The Chambers of Edwin James, Q.C. and the Steps of the Garrick Club

Yates, endowed with the virtues that are much in need by the gossip columnist—aggression and love of battle—sought an opinion of counsel as to the right of the Club to eject him and to erase his name from the Club roster. Gordon Ray, Thackeray's modern biographer, passes over this phase of the Garrick Club Controversy as "tedious to trace." It is hard to agree with his judgment, in view of the ironic literary overtones of the legal maneuvers in behalf of Yates.

The strategy of Edwin James, Q.C., whom Yates consulted, was sound both from the legal and Dickensian point of view—he sought to prevent Yates's case from following the dismal course of *Jarndyce* v. *Jarndyce*, the eternal Chancery proceeding made famous by Dickens in *Bleak House* (which had appeared six years earlier). James advised that the case be shaped to fall within the traditional common-law tort category of trespass. Plans were made to file the action against the secretary of the Club as the delegate of the Club's trustees authorized to commit the tort. Yates arranged that the secretary would meet him at the front door of the Club and eject him. Yates turned up at the foreordained time accompanied by his solicitor, and on his saying to the secretary that he must enter, the secretary "replied good-humouredly, 'I suppose this is what you want Mr. Yates—will this do?' and laid his hand on my shoulder, to prevent my going further." Despite the fact that this charade at the Club-door was a worthy successor to such earlier English legal ceremonies as delivery of the peppercorn, and the fine and common recovery, the polite trespass was ineffective. The court held that Yates's sole remedy was against the Club trustees, who could be pursued only in the Court of Chancery. Although Yates's solicitor replied cheerfully, on inquiry, that the cost of a Chancery proceeding would probably not be more than £200 or £300, this did not strike the young Yates as a great bargain. He dropped the case.

However, creative men may find a rich lode in others' misfortunes. Yates took Dickens to one of his consultations with Edwin James. While the "fat, florid" James tried vainly to be "specially agreeable," Dickens was "quietly observant." The observation was to transform James into the lawyer Mr. Stryver of *A Tale of Two Cities*, "a man of little more than thirty, but looking twenty years older, stout, loud, red, bluff and free from any drawback of delicacy; [who] had a very pushing way of shouldering himself, morally and physically, into companies and conversations that argued well for his shouldering his way up in life."

In November, 1858, while the legal battles were still in mid-course, Dickens returned to London after an absence of several months on a lecture tour. Following up "six words" he had said to Thackeray at the Athenaeum when he last saw him, Dickens wrote a letter to Thackeray in which he belatedly made what appears to have been a sincere attempt to end the quarrel, as he had years before succeeded in doing in Thackeray's feud with Forster. Perhaps it is a signal of their growing estrangement that Dickens preferred to follow up his brief introduction of the subject by correspondence instead of in a face-to-face meeting with his old comrade. In any event, the tone of Dickens's letter was not warm, and its author made two crucial blunders. First, Dickens referred to the retention of Edwin James and to the opinion of that legal worthy that the expulsion of Yates was unlawful. Still worse, he made reference to his own previous consultation with Yates. Dickens proceeded to inquire whether a conference could be held for the purpose of reaching "some quiet accommodation of this deplorable matter." But even in making this tardy initiative, Dickens maintained his alignment with Yates's side—he did not offer direct mediation between the adversaries but proposed that he meet as a representative of Yates with an "appointed friend of yours, as representing you." What an insulting suggestion this must have been to Thackeray, to have his peer and supposed friend persevere in the role of second to an unworthy opponent! Dickens ended his letter with the suggestion that if the proposed meeting could not take place, his letter and Thackeray's reply should be burned. Thackeray's letter of reply was brusque. He "grieved" to note that Dickens had been Yates's adviser in the dispute and further did not believe that the Club would be frightened by the opinion of any lawyer. To emphasize his full rejection of Dickens's overture, Thackeray, instead of burning the correspondence as suggested, delivered copies to the Club. He subscribed his letter to Dickens rudely, "Yours, &c, W. M. Thackeray." The break between the two men was now complete. But perhaps Thackeray had from the very beginning fancied he saw the hand of Dickens behind the controversy. Taxed by a young friend with forgetting his dignity in condescending to quarrel with the insignificant Yates, Thackeray responded: "You may not think, young 'un, that I am quarreling with Mr. Yates. I am hitting the man behind him."

And so it was that Edmund Yates, a literary pygmy, was expelled from the Garrick Club, leaving behind him a shattered friendship of two giants.

Act Three, Scene Two: The Athenaeum Club

Lovers of Dickens and Thackeray are grateful that the two men were ultimately reconciled. The reconciliation, like the feud, had its setting at a club. The initiative appears to have come from Thackeray. In the spring of 1863 Thackeray told Katey Dickens (with whom he had remained on friendly terms) that it was ridiculous that Dickens and he "should be placed in a position of enmity towards one another," but added that he could not apologize: "You know," he said, "he is more in the wrong than I am." The diplomatic Katey replied that Thackeray should nevertheless make the first move since her father was "more shy of speaking than are you." Later that year (possibly in May) Thackeray saw Dickens at the Athenaeum Club and held out his hand to him, saying: "We have been foolish long enough," and Dickens grasped his hand "very cordially."

In December Thackeray died and Dickens stood at the graveside of his great rival. Thackeray's last visit to his beloved Garrick Club was made during the last week of his life. His friend Shirley Brooks fittingly included an account of the visit in his obituary in *Punch*:

> On the Tuesday he came to his favorite club, 'The Garrick', and asked for a seat at the table of two friends, who, of course, welcomed him, as all welcomed Thackeray. It will not be deemed too minute a record by any of the hundreds who personally loved him, to note where he sat for the last time at that club. There is in the dining-room in the first floor a nook near the reading-room. . . . [Here] Thackeray took his seat, and dined with his friends. He was afterwards in the smoke-room, a place in which he delighted. . . . Before the dawn of Thursday he was where there was no night.

Epilogue: Hyères, France

With Thackeray's death, one of the three protagonists of the Unpleasantness at the Garrick Club was gone. A few notes must be added on the other actors in the drama before the final curtain falls.

Dickens, who, as we have seen, had resigned from the Garrick Club twice before, tendered his final resignation in 1865, enraged over the blackballing of his friend and subeditor, W. H. Wills. Percy Fitzgerald observes respectfully that Dickens no doubt found the enjoyments of the Club incompatible with his work.

Edmund Yates continued his career of gossip and scandal. That he delighted in conflict is suggested by lines from Tennyson's *Ulysses*, which Yates chose as the epigraph for his *Recollections and Experiences* published in 1884:

> Much have I seen and known: cities of men
> And manners, climates, councils, governments,
> And drunk delight of battle with my peers.

His fellow journalist Harry Furniss writes that "Yates was, perhaps, the most hated man in town, for which his repulsive manner and repellent pen must be held to account." Furniss adds reassuringly, "Personally, I liked Yates."

In 1883 Yates was prosecuted criminally for libel against the Earl of

Lonsdale in an article commenting on the "Yellow Earl's" romance with the stage beauty Violet Cameron. Yates served seven weeks of a four-month prison sentence. When the news of Yates's conviction reached Robert Louis Stevenson in Hyères, France, Stevenson was so happy that he ordered a bonfire to be built in his garden and he, Fanny and their maid danced madly around it hand in hand. Typically, the exertion proved too much for Stevenson and he took to his bed for days.

Curtain

"Under Sentence of Death": Some Literary Views on Capital Punishment

One of the most fiercely contested fronts of the continuing conflict over capital punishment in the United States is statistical. In the case of *Gregg* v. *Georgia*, the Supreme Court of the United States was asked to decide issues of life and death on the basis of econometric studies of Prof. Isaac Ehrlich that concluded, contrary to earlier findings, that capital punishment has a deterrent effect on murder and that "an additional execution per year over the period in question [1933–1969] may have resulted, on average, in 7 or 8 fewer murders." In the winter of 1975–76 the *Yale Law Journal* published critiques of Ehrlich's work, together with his rejoinders, and strong words were exchanged about the appropriateness of statistical "regression" analysis to criminal conduct, the accuracy of Professor Ehrlich's theories as to the variables influencing the murder rate, the quality of his data, and the validity of his statistical technique.

The decision of the Supreme Court in *Gregg*, 428 U.S. 153 (1976), did not resolve the controversy. While holding that capital punishment was not under all circumstances "cruel and unusual," the Court rejected the statistical studies on deterrence as "inconclusive." However, the majority opinion stated that for some murderers "the death penalty undoubtedly is a deterrent"; and that "retribution," the second principal "social purpose" of the death penalty, is neither "a forbidden objective nor one inconsistent with our respect for the dignity of man."

There is a distinctly American flavor to the econometric debate over deterrence. As Dwight MacDonald pointed out many years ago in his essay *The Triumph of the Fact*, Americans are enamored of statistics whether they relate to batting averages or to major political or social issues. Ironically, it does not appear likely that Professor Ehrlich's conclusions, even if confirmed by further research, will be a decisive influence on the judgments the courts and the state legislatures must make on the retention or abolition of capital punishment. Prof. Jon K. Peck, in trying to moderate the opposed views of Ehrlich and his critics, has pointed out the relative insignificance of capital punishment as a deterrent even under Ehrlich's own equations: a one percent change in per capita income produces a greater effect on the homicide rate than a one percent increase in the number of executions. Professor Ehrlich has himself emphasized that he has not advocated the use of capital punishment and that "the issue of deterrence is but one of a myriad of issues relating to the efficiency and desirability of capital punishment as a social instrument for combating crime."

Therefore, as we await further reports from the statisticians, we will continue, as our ancestors have done, to listen to other voices on the issues of capital punishment. Those who take some guidance from the minds and hearts of our great writers will find that the literature of capital punishment is a primary source to be consulted.

The Eighteenth Century

The eighteenth century was for the English a heyday of crime and the Golden Age of Deterrence. England's so-called "Bloody Code" (which was not adopted in the American Colonies) imposed the death penalty for hundreds of crimes from murder to trivial shopliftings. The frequent public hangings which were carried out in London in the name of deterrence did nothing to stem an enormous tide of violent crimes and thefts, and appeared to serve the principal function of public amusement, not only for the working classes (who were generally given a holiday on "hanging day") but for the educated as well. The same age that produced this savagery also gave us Henry Fielding and Samuel Johnson.

Henry Fielding, who is known to us all as the author of *Tom Jones*, is remembered in the history of criminal law as a tough-minded and compassionate justice of the peace of Middlesex County and the City of Westminster (Greater London). Regarded as a founder, with his blind brother John, of London's police force, Fielding was faced with a terrible conflict between his recognition of the inhumanity of the frequent executions under the "Bloody Code," and his abiding faith that capital punishment, properly applied, could have a deterrent effect on the rising crime rate.

Fielding set down his thoughts on criminal punishment in his treatise

An Enquiry Into the Causes of the Late Increase of Robbers (1751). Quoting Lord Hale, he postulated that the principal end of all punishment was less to punish for past offenses than to "deter men from the breach of laws, so that they may not offend and so not suffer at all." The humane goal of punishment then was to make punishment unnecessary at some point in the utopian future. Only with that hope in his heart could Fielding be reconciled to the infliction of capital punishment for petty thefts, for "no man indeed of common humanity or common sense can think the life of a man and a few shillings to be of an equal consideration, or that the law in punishing theft with death proceeds (as perhaps a private person sometimes may) with any view to vengeance. The terror of the example is the only thing proposed, and one man is sacrificed to the preservation of thousands."

And so the kindly Fielding set about the task of proposing how the terror of punishment could be maximized. First, the sovereign must renounce his prerogative of mercy and decline to pardon criminals under death sentence, for "pardons have brought many more men to the gallows than they have saved." Second, reforms must be introduced into the manner of execution, since a convicted thief, far from fearing death, often viewed his execution as a source of glory rather than shame, and the procession to the gallows at Tyburn (the site of the modern Marble Arch) as a triumph.

The greatest cause of the convict's bravado Fielding found in the very frequency of executions in the city—"the thief who is hanged to-day hath learned his intrepidity from the example of his hanged predecessors." The design of those who made executions public had been to add the punishment of shame to that of death, but experience had been contrary: the mob found diversion and the convict an easy heroism. One way of preventing frequency of executions was to attack the roots of crime, and Fielding in his treatise suggested a broad store of remedies— restraint of the passion for luxury, drunkenness and gambling; improvement of provision for the poor; stricter punishment of receivers of stolen goods; and improved administration of criminal justice.

While these goals were being pursued, the performance of executions should be modified. Executions should not be delayed so long that public resentment of the crime cooled and that the punishment itself became the sole subject of contemplation. "No good mind," Fielding wrote, "can avoid compassionating a set of wretches who are put to death we know not why, unless, as it almost appears, to make a holiday for, and to entertain, the mob." He also proposed that executions be to "some degree private" so that, taking added intensity from the imaginations of the excluded public, they could assume the terror of the off-stage murders of classical drama. Terror should also be heightened,

Fielding wrote, by giving execution the highest degree of solemnity. He suggested that at the end of the trials the Court of Old Bailey be adjourned for four days; that a gallows be erected in the area before the court; and that all the convicted criminals be brought down together to receive sentence and be executed forthwith in the presence of their judges. Fielding had little room for appellate courts in his scheme of things.

Samuel Johnson, unlike Fielding, announced himself an enemy of those who tinkered with the time-honored festival of public hanging. In 1783, he lamented to Sir William Scott the abolition of the procession to the hanging site at Tyburn:

> The age is running mad after innovation; and all the business of the world is to be done in a new way; men are to be hanged in a new way; Tyburn itself is not safe from the fury of innovation. . . . it is *not* an improvement; they object, that the old method drew together a number of spectators. Sir, executions are intended to draw spectators. If they do not draw spectators, they don't answer their purpose. The old method was most satisfactory to all parties; the publick was gratified by a procession; the criminal was supported by it. Why is all this to be swept away?

Perhaps Dr. Johnson was speaking in jest, but he appeared to be saying that the public found Tyburn more entertaining than terrifying. Abolitionists often quote his comment that he had seen pickpockets working the crowd around the gallows though their trade was punished by hanging. In any event, Johnson's mind was so palatial that it echoed with inconsistencies. He displayed his delightful ability to take every side of an issue in his comments on the effect of a prospective execution on the mind of condemned criminals. In 1769 Boswell mentioned to him that he had seen the execution of several convicts at Tyburn and that none of them seemed to be under any concern. "Most of them, Sir," Johnson explained, "have never thought at all." This observation hardly provides a psychological basis for the eighteenth-century belief that prospective criminals may be deterred by the risk of execution. However, in speaking of the forthcoming execution of the clergyman Rev. Dodd for forgery, Johnson took an opposite position in his famous quip: "Depend upon it, Sir, when a man knows that he is to be hanged in a fortnight, it concentrates his mind wonderfully."

The efforts Johnson made in the unsuccessful campaign to save Dodd from the gallows may show more clearly where his heart lay on the use of capital punishment—at least in cases of nonviolent crime—than do his casual comments to his friends. He drafted Dodd's speech before sentencing at the Old Bailey, petitions of Dodd and his wife to the king and queen, and even a farewell address to Dodd's fellow convicts.

In the appeal to the king that Johnson wrote for Dr. Dodd, he begged that the sentence be commuted to exile and referred to the "horrour and ignominy of a publick execution" and to "the spectacle of a clergyman dragged through the streets, to a death of infamy, amidst the derision of the profligate and the profane." Johnson sought no credit for his humane intervention but on the contrary enjoined Dodd to keep secret his authorship of the numerous petitions and letters he had written for the prisoner.

The Nineteenth Century

Literary history also tells us that Gary Gilmore was far from the first condemned man to announce a preference for execution over imprisonment. A melodramatic precedent was recorded by Frances Trollope in her comments on an execution in Cincinnati in *Domestic Manners of the Americans* (1832). A great throng assembled for the hanging, not for traditional merrymaking as in eighteenth- or nineteenth-century London but to witness a novelty, for Mrs. Trollope notes that her informants told her no white man had ever been executed at Cincinnati. The convict, who had been condemned on the testimony of his own son, turned down an offer of reprieve from the governor of Ohio, saying to the sheriff, "If any thing could make me agree to it, it would be the hope of living long enough to kill you and my dog of a son: however, I won't agree; you shall have the hanging of me." The sheriff on the day of execution assumed his alternate office of hangman, but with his watch in one hand and in his other the knife for cutting the rope, made one last effort to obtain the criminal's acceptance of the offered commutation. Unlike Gilmore, the Ohio convict had a last minute change of heart, and when "the hand was lifted to strike, . . . the criminal stoutly exclaimed, 'I sign'; and he was conveyed back to prison, amidst the shouts, laughter, and ribaldry of the mob." Mrs. Trollope concluded: "I am not fond of hanging, but there was something in all this that did not look like the decent dignity of wholesome justice."

In the early nineteenth century a group of law reformers led by Sir Samuel Romilly mounted an attack on England's Bloody Code that finally succeeded in reducing the number of capital provisions from over 200 to 15. The battle for the absolute abolition of capital punishment was to be waged for the next century and a half. Among the outstanding voices raised in the cause of abolition during the Victorian period were those of Dickens and Thackeray.

Thackeray anticipated Dickens's more famous abolitionist writings by several years. Thackeray's essays on the death penalty, which I discuss in a chapter of *Innocence and Arsenic: Studies in Crime and Literature*, were the product of a highly personal blend of morbid fascination with public hanging and an intense, almost hypochondriacal empathy with the hanged man. His 1839 article on the execution of Sebastian Peytel, which he had unsuccessfully sought to attend, presents many of his principal arguments against the death penalty. First of all, Thackeray, like Balzac who had also interested himself in the case, was not sure that Peytel was guilty of the murder with which he was charged. He urged that we should "at least, be sure of a man's guilt before we murder him." In his peroration against the execution of Peytel, Thackeray forcibly put other arguments: that the execution does not deter others from crimes and is a source of entertainment rather than moral profit; and that imprisonment is an adequate alternative means of protection of society.

The scope of Thackeray's opposition to capital punishment widened in his *On Going to See a Man Hanged* (1840) written after he finally attended a hanging (of the murderer Courvoisier) and found he could not bring himself to look. The question of doubtful guilt did not now condition his views since the hanged man's guilt was conceded. But Thackeray's strong personal identification with Courvoisier was now supported by the insight that hanging was pornographic: that it brutalized the public by appealing to its sensual instincts. He was left with "an extraordinary feeling of terror and shame," springing from his partaking with 40,000 others in "this hideous debauchery, which is more exciting than sleep, or than wine, or the last new ballet."

Thackeray and Dickens saw each other in the crowd at Courvoisier's hanging but neither could catch the other's eye. Dickens did not react to the sight with the emotional immediacy of Thackeray. Indeed, public executions continued to exert on him what he called the "attraction of repulsion." Philip Collins in his admirable work *Dickens and Crime* has defended Dickens against the charge of being a "masculine Madame Defarge," but the fact is that he attended three or possibly four executions. Thackeray, so far as we know, gave up death as a spectator sport after the Courvoisier execution, and once turned down an invitation to a foreign beheading, commenting, "*j'y ai été* [I've been there already], as the Frenchman said of hunting."

Despite the ambivalence of the emotions that were stirred by Dickens's observation of executions, the Courvoisier hanging undoubtedly had a great impact on his conscience. He recalled the scene vividly six years later in the first of a series of four long articles to the *Daily News* in which he advocated the total abolition of capital punishment. He wrote of the effect of the execution on the crowd in attendance: "No sorrow, no salutary terror, no abhorrence, no seriousness; nothing but ribaldry, debauchery, levity, drunkenness, and flaunting vice in fifty other shapes. I should have deemed it impossible that I could have ever felt any large assemblage of my fellow-creatures to be so odious." In his arguments against capital punishment, Dickens emphasized as had Thackeray its tendency to barbarize and desensitize the community. He also quoted several examples of hangings of the innocent, including a report of a New York Select Committee. (Six years later in *Bleak House* Dickens satirized the desire of the public to see murder avenged by the execution of *somebody* regardless of guilt or innocence: the "debilitated cousin" opines to Inspector Bucket in his slurring style that he "hasn't a doubt—zample—far better hang wrong fler [fellow] than no fler.") Dickens also cited statistics that abolition of the death penalty in certain foreign countries had not led to increases in their murder rates. As an additional blow to the deterrence theory, he cited a favorite statistic of abolitionists: that according to a prison chaplain in Bristol, only 3 of the 167 prisoners he had attended under sentence of death had not been spectators at public executions.

The uniqueness of Dickens's articles, however, lies not in the assembling of these arguments but in the application of his fictive imagination to the potentially harmful role of the gallows in shaping the evil resolves of the would-be murderer. He noted that for the murderer with exhibitionistic instincts the death penalty and its attendant notoriety, far from acting as a deterrent, in fact provide an incentive. The "ill-regulated mind" of the murderer actuated by revenge, Dickens argued further, might impel him to kill on the basis of the mechanistic calculation that capital punishment, by demanding life as the price of a life, had removed the "base and cowardly character of murder" and that society by hanging him would receive its just bargain. Pursuing this line of thought, Dickens feared that the prospect of hanging might also incite the wife-murderer who could feel that his crime was not the cowardly slaughter of a woman but a heroic challenge to the shadow of the gallows and a response to its dark fascination: "Present this black idea of violence to a bad mind contemplating violence; hold up before a man remotely compassing the death of another person, the spectacle of his own ghastly and untimely death by man's hands; and out of the depths of his own nature you shall assuredly raise up that which lures and tempts him on." Later in the forties Dickens abandoned his advocacy of total abolition of capital punishment, but passionately urged an end to public hanging in his famous letters to *The Times* which were inspired by the obscene behavior of the crowd at the hangings of Frederick and Maria Manning.

Dickens emphasized that his writings against capital punishment and public hanging were not inspired by sympathy for the criminal, whom he claimed (in an article against flogging) to hold "in far lower estimation than a mad wolf." It was as a novelist rather than as a wavering abolitionist that Dickens taught most persuasively that the passion to save and conserve life is a communal force that binds and enhances society however worthless may be the individual whose life is saved. In *Our Mutual Friend*, a doctor, with the help of four tough habitués of a riverside tavern, does his human best to revive the villainous Rogue Riderhood, who has fallen into the Thames. The onlookers are rewarded by a sign of returning life in a man they despised before and would despise again: "See! A token of life! An indubitable token of life! The spark may smoulder and go out or it may glow and expand, but see! The four rough fellows seeing, shed tears. Neither Riderhood in this world, nor Riderhood in the other could drag tears from them; but a striving human soul between the two can do it easily." This passage can do much to explain how many people can favor capital punishment in principle but hope it will never be applied, or struggle to save a Gary Gilmore from an overdose, though knowing that in another room a firing squad will claim him.

The Twentieth Century

Prior to World War II George Orwell made a poignant contribution to the literature of capital punishment with *A Hanging* (1931), his eyewitness description of an execution in a Burmese prison yard. Recreating the horror of the scene with a novelist's eye for cumulative physical detail—the last-minute incursion of a prancing half Airedale, the "bobbing gait" of the slight Indian prisoner on his way to the gallows, his reiterated prayer cry of "Ram! Ram! Ram!" answered by the howls of the dog—Orwell recalled a minute action of the convict that brought home to him the meaning of what was being done. During the procession to the place of execution, in spite of the tight grasp of two warders, the condemned man "stepped slightly aside to avoid a puddle on the path." Orwell, who "had never realized what it means to destroy a healthy, conscious man," now saw "the mystery, the unspeakable wrongness, of cutting a life short, when it is in full tide." He wrote of the prisoner during that last walk: "His eyes saw the yellow gravel and the grey walls, and his brain still remembered, foresaw, reasoned—even about puddles. He and we were a party of men walking together, seeing, hearing, feeling, understanding the same world; and in two minutes, with a sudden snap, one of us would be gone—one mind less, one world less."

After the war two works urging abolition of the death penalty were published in this country by influential European writers, Arthur Koestler's *Reflections on Hanging* and Albert Camus' *Reflections on the Guillotine*. Both writers were inspired by traumatic personal experience. "In 1937, during the Civil War in Spain," Koestler wrote in his preface, "I spent three months under sentence of death as a suspected spy, witnessing the executions of my fellow prisoners and awaiting my own." Camus recalled that when he was a child his father arose in the dark to attend the execution of a brutal murderer who had slaughtered an entire family of farmers. One of the few things Camus knew about his father was that this was the first time he had wanted to witness a guillotining. He never forgot his mother's account of his father's return:

> He never told what he saw that morning. My mother could only report that he rushed wildly into the house, refused to speak, threw himself on the bed, and suddenly began to vomit. He had just discovered the reality concealed beneath the great formulas that ordinarily serve to mask it. Instead of thinking of the murdered children, he could recall only the trembling body he had seen thrown on a board to have its head chopped off.

Koestler's book (unlike Camus' shorter essay which relied on Koestler for much of its factual foundation) is in large part a history of the development and function of capital punishment. As Dickens and other nineteenth-century predecessors had done, Koestler devotes many pages to showing that the deterrent effect of the death penalty has not been established and that there has been a discouraging number of judicial errors in capital cases. Koestler's sketch of the growth of the Bloody Code in eighteenth-century England is illuminating. He points out the paradox (which he regards as relevant to the dialogue on punishments which continues in our time) that the English opted for more and more severe penalties because they feared that the alternative of a stronger and more efficient police system posed a greater threat to their freedoms.

The heart of Koestler's argument for abolition is philosophic. Rejecting the validity of the deterrence theory, he concludes that the force behind retention of the death penalty is a desire for vengeance: "Deep inside every civilized being there lurks a tiny Stone Age man, dangling a club to rob and rape, and screaming an eye for an eye. But we would rather not have that little fur-clad figure dictate the law of the land." Koestler rejected retribution not only emotionally but also on the basis of principles of moral philosophy. He observed that neither religion nor philosophy had ever resolved the question whether man is moved to act by free will or predetermination. If murder was blindly predetermined by heredity, environment or other factors, Koestler argued, "vengeance against a human being is as absurd as punishing a machine." On the other hand, even the acceptance of freedom of the will left unanswered "the problem of evil: the fact that evil has been included in the [higher] design." In sentencing for all offenses other than murder, the administrators of the law could compromise with the determinist view by finding gradations of culpability and letting the punishment fit the crime. But Koestler pointed out that the death penalty left no room for compromise. Its "rigidity and finality" presupposed an absolute criminal responsibility which philosophical concepts did not support.

Camus' arguments are less abstract and to me much more moving. He begins, perhaps with a degree of irony, by parting company with the reformers since Fielding: if we really mean business about deterrence, we should guillotine in public so that we will all be confronted with the horrible actuality of execution rather than reading the euphemistic death reports in the morning papers while downing our coffee. Public execution was necessary if the guillotine was to make an example, Camus argued, but he doubted that it deterred either the crime of passion or those who lived by crime. In that crowd in which Camus' father stood "there must have been a considerable number of future criminals who did not run home and vomit." It could not be denied that men fear death, but Camus believed such fear could be overmastered by human passion or neutralized by the criminal's instinctual optimism— that he will not be caught, will not be found guilty, will not be sentenced to death, or will not be executed.

Rejecting the deterrent function of the guillotine, Camus brands it a form of revenge that is "as old as man himself, and usually goes by the name of *retaliation*." But capital punishment more than matches murder, he adds. Rarely does murder have the degree of cold premeditation or impose such agonized waiting in which "torture by hope alternates only with the pangs of animal despair." If there were to be a real equivalence, "the death penalty would have to be pronounced upon a criminal who had forewarned his victim of the very moment he would put him to a horrible death, and who, from that time on, had kept him confined at his own discretion for a period of months. It is not in private life that one meets such monsters."

Camus tests the strength of his own belief in abolition by raising the question whether he would forbid application of the death penalty to "irrecoverables" such as mass murderers. Even in this case he decides against capital punishment, fearing judicial error (as in the case of Marie Besnard) or the pressures of public opinion (as in cases of terrorist acts judged in the light of "accidents of the times . . . and of geography"). But even "monsters" he would not subject to the "absolute" punishment of death since there is no absolute innocence. As a matter of logic he would deny to no man the right of reparation by his later life in a secularized world which has lost faith in the possibility of redemption beyond the grave.

Camus' ultimate arguments are social and political. Capital punishment is wrong in Camus' view because it "destroys the human community united against death" (a community Dickens had sketched in small as the four men cheered by the revival of Rogue Riderhood). Moreover, our civilization defines itself, Camus concludes, by the fact that "for thirty years crimes of State have vastly exceeded crimes of individuals" not only through war but also political killings. He urges that the abolition of the death penalty is the first step in the denial of the right of the State to destroy its citizens.

Postscript: The "Perfect" Death

The literature of capital punishment often dwells on the clumsiness of the tools of death. We read of the headsmen who missed; of the (almost literally) immortal Half Hanged Smith; of the ingeniously contrived "new drop" which was new but did not drop; of the electric chairs with defective circuiting. Doubts continue, we are told, that even the guillotine brings instant oblivion, and at least a qualm of credulity is aroused by the tale that the cheek of the severed head of Charlotte Corday, when slapped by the assistant executioner, flared with indignation. If one's mind is in close balance on the death penalty, it is tempting to divert the issue of "cruel and unusual punishment" from the fact of death to the means of killing. One might even become nostalgic over the days when a cup of hemlock was passed to troublesome philosophers. But death, however painless, remains the issue. John Webster's Duchess of Malfi reminded her executioner of this when he attempted to terrify her with the sight of her own coffin and the cord with which she was to be strangled:

> What would it pleasure me to have my throat cut
> With diamonds? or to be smothered
> With cassia? or to be shot to death with pearls?

Bibliographical Notes

The Ring and the Book and the Murder

For quotations from *The Ring and the Book* and line references, I have used the edition by Richard D. Altick in the English Poets series (New Haven, 1971).

I have read two English translations of the collection of trial documents on which the book is based, the so-called "Old Yellow Book": those of Charles W. Hodell in the Everyman's Library; and of John Marshall Gest (Philadelphia 1927). The Gest edition reorganizes and groups the arguments and counterarguments in logical legal sequence, and includes annotations summarizing the cited authorities. Certain supplementary documents relating to the case are published in *Curious Annals*, translated, edited, and with an introduction by Beatrice Corrigan (Toronto, 1956).

Subsequent to the original publication of my article in 1966, the first full-length literary study of *The Ring and the Book* appeared: Richard D. Altick and James F. Loucks II, *Browning's Roman Murder Story* (Chicago, 1968).

My quotations from G. K. Chesterton are from his *Robert Browning* (London 1951), pp. 160, 168.

Portraits of Beatrice: The Cenci Case in Literature and Opera

A detailed historical account of the Cenci case is provided by Corrado Ricci, *The Story of Beatrice Cenci*, translated by Morris Bishop and Henry Longan Stuart (New York, 1933). See also Antonio Bertolotti, *Francesco Cenci e la sua Famiglia* (Florence, 1877).

The principal literary versions of the Cenci case discussed are:

Artaud, Antonin. *The Cenci.* Translated by Simon Watson Taylor. New York, 1970.

Browning, Robert. "Cenciaja." In *The Poems and Plays of Robert Browning.* Modern Library edition. New York: n.d. Pp. 1008–12.

Dumas, Alexandre. "The Cenci." In *Celebrated Crimes.* Translated by I. G. Burnham. 8 vols. Philadelphia, 1895. Vol. 5, pp. 3–47.

Guerrazzi, Francesco. *Beatrice Cenci.* Translated by Luigi Monti. Published by the National Alumni, 1907.

Hawthorne, Nathaniel. *The Marble Faun.* 2 vols. Boston, 1891. Vol. 1, chapter 7.

Landor, Walter Savage. *Five Scenes.* In *The Poetical Works of Walter Savage Landor.* 3 vols. Edited by Stephen Wheeler. Oxford, 1937. Vol. 2, pp. 6–29.

Moravia, Alberto. *Beatrice Cenci.* Translated by Angus Davidson. New York, 1966.

Prokosch, Frederic. *A Tale for Midnight.* New York, 1956.

Shand, William, and Girri, Alberto. *Beatrix Cenci.* Libretto for opera in two acts and fourteen scenes by Alberto Ginastera. New York, 1971.

Shelley, Percy Bysshe. "The Cenci." In *John Keats and Percy Bysshe Shelley: Complete Poetical Works.* Modern Library edition. New York, n.d. Pp. 298–366.

Stendhal (Marie-Henri Beyle). *The Cenci.* In *The Shorter Novels of Stendhal.* Translated by C. K. Scott-Moncrieff. New York, 1946. Pp. 165–203.

Thackeray, William Makepeace. "Celebrated Crimes." In *The New Sketch Book.* Edited by Robert S. Garnett. London, 1906. Pp. 86–87.

For the description of the style of Słowacki's *Beatrix Cenci,* see Stefan Treugott, *Julius Słowacki, Romantic Poet* (Warsaw, 1959), p. 88.

Innocence and Arsenic: The Literary and Criminal Careers of C. J. L. Almquist

I have read the following Swedish editions of the principal works of Almquist discussed in the article:

Amorina, eller Historien om de Fyra [*Amorina, or The History of the Four*]. Stockholm, 1903.

Det går an [*It Will Do*]. Edited by Sune Martinson. Stockholm, 1965.

Drottningens juvelsmycke, eller Azouras Lazuli Tintomara [*The Queen's Jewel, or Azouras Lazuli Tintomara*]. With a foreword by Bertil Romberg. Stockholm, 1966.

Det går an is available in English translation under the title *Sara Videbeck,* translated by Adolph Burnett Benson (New York, 1972).

For an account of the trial of Almquist, see A. Hemming-Sjöberg, *A Poet's Tragedy,* translated by E. Classen (London, 1932). Additional biographical and critical sources are:

Böök, Fredrik. *Analys och Porträtt.* Stockholm, 1962. Pp. 151–63.

Olsson, Henry. *Törnrosdiktaren och andra porträtt* [*The Poet of the Briar Rose and Other Portraits*]. Stockholm, 1956. Pp. 35–213.

Romberg, Bertil. *Carl Jonas Love Almqvist.* Translated by Sten Lidén. Boston, 1977.

Schück, Henrik and Warburg, Karl. *Illusterad Svensk Litteraturhistoria.* 8 vols. 3rd completely revised edition. Stockholm, 1926–49. Vol. 6, pp. 231–374.

For studies of the Attarp and Lafarge murder cases, respectively, see Yngve Lyttkens, *Attarpsmorden* (Stockholm, 1953); and Edith Saunders, *The Mystery of Marie Lafarge* (New York, 1952).

Strict Construction in Sung China: The Case of A Yün

The principal accounts of the case of A Yün are found in Shen Chia-pen, *Bequeathed Writings,* Vol. 24, chapter 4, pp. 15 et seq., and Wilhelm, Helmut, "Der Prozess der A Yün," *Monumenta Serica* I: 338–51 (1935).

Other works that I have consulted are:

Alabaster, Ernest. *Notes and Commentaries on Chinese Criminal Law.* London, 1899.

Bodde, Derk, and Morris, Clarence. *Law in Imperial China.* Cambridge, Mass., 1967.

Cohen, Jerome Alan. *The Criminal Process in the People's Republic of China 1949–1963: An Introduction.* Cambridge, Mass., 1968.

Kracke, E. A., Jr. *Civil Service in Early Sung China 960–1067.* Cambridge, Mass., 1968.

Lin Yutang. *The Gay Genius.* New York, 1947.

Liu, James T. C. *Reform in Sung China: Wang An-shih (1021–1086) and His New Policies.* Cambridge, Mass., 1959.

Manuel du code chinois. Translated by G. Boulais. Taipei, 1966. Sections 115–25.

Shu Ching (Book of History). Edited by Clae Waltham. Chicago, 1971.

Ta Tsing Leu Lee. Translated by Sir George Thomas Staunton. Taipei, 1966.

Van Gulik, R. H. *Parallel Cases from under the Peartree.* Leiden, 1956.

Williamson, H. R. *Wang An-Shih,* 2 vols. London, 1935.

"The Sinister Behind the Ordinary": Emlyn Williams's *Night Must Fall*

Studies of the murder cases on which Emlyn Williams drew in *Night Must Fall* may be found in the following sources:

Patrick Mahon: Wallace, Edgar. *The Trial of Patrick Herbert Mahon.* Famous Trials Series. New York, 1928.

Toni Mancini: Hyde, H. Montgomery. *Lord Justice: The Life and Times of Lord Birkett of Ulverston.* New York, 1965. Pp. 394–418.

Henry Jacoby: Allen, Trevor. "The Lady White Murder." In *Famous Crimes of Recent Times.* London, n.d. Pp. 52–67.

John Donald Merrett: Trial of John Donald Merrett. Edited by William Roughead. Notable British Trials. Edinburgh, 1929.

Sidney Harry Fox: Trial of Sidney Harry Fox. Edited by F. Tennyson Jesse. Notable British Trials. Edinburgh, 1934.

The Le Touquet case: Stern, G. B. "The Le Touquet Mystery." In *Great Unsolved Crimes*. London, n.d. [1935]. Pp. 197–204.

For F. Tennyson Jesse's concept of the "murderee," see her *Murder and Its Motives*, new edition (London, 1952), pp. 60–62.

Biographical information regarding Williams is drawn from his *Emlyn: An early autobiography 1927–1935* (London 1973), and also from his Introduction to his *Collected Plays*, vol. 1 (London, 1961), pp. xv–xix.

This essay first appeared in somewhat different form as a program note for the Cleveland Play House's production of *Night Must Fall*, starring Margaret Hamilton (October 13–November 18, 1978).

Emlyn Williams later in his career produced other works based on actual crimes: his play *Someone Waiting* (1953) inspired by the trial of Brian Donald Hume, and *Beyond Belief* (1967), an idiosyncratic but often moving account of the Moors Murder Case.

Lully and the Death of Cambert

Historical Background

The Gluck-Piccinni rivalry is discussed in Alfred Einstein, *Gluck*, translated by Eric Blom (New York, 1962), pp. 162–69. For an analysis of the tradition of Mozart's murder, see my "Salieri and the 'Murder' of Mozart," in *Innocence and Arsenic: Studies in Crime and Literature* (New York, 1977), pp. 63–86. An excellent description of the cultural centralism which fostered Lully's control over French opera is provided in Robert M. Isherwood, *Music in the Service of the King: France in the Seventeenth Century* (Ithaca, 1973).

Music History

The two principal theoretical works contrasting the French and Italian styles as developed in the late seventeenth century were Raguenet's *Parallèle des Italiens et des Français* (1702) and Le Cerf de la Viéville's *Comparaison de la musique italienne et de la musique française* (1705). The best biographical works on Lully are those by Henry Prunières: *Lully* (Paris, 1909), and the fictionalized *La Vie Illustre et Libertine de Jean-Baptiste Lully* (Paris, 1929). Later biographies appear to be highly derivative from Prunières, e.g., R. H. F. Scott, *Jean-Baptiste Lully: The Founder of French Opera* (London, 1973); Eugène Borrel, *Jean-Baptiste Lully* (Paris, 1949). For appraisals of Cambert's contributions to French opera, see Arthur Pougin, *Les Vrais Créateurs de l'Opéra Français: Perrin et Cambert* (Paris, 1881); Charles Nuitter et Ernest Thoinan, *Les Origines de l'Opéra Français* (Paris, 1886). References to Cambert's career in London are drawn from André Tessier, "Robert Cambert à Londres," *La Revue Musicale*, December 1927, pp. 101, 110–11, 118; W. H. Grattan Flood, "Quelques précisions nouvelles sur Cambert et Grabu à Londres," *La Revue Musicale*, August 1928, p. 351.

The Lully-Cambert Rumors

The posthumous tribute to Lully referred to is *Le triomphe de Lully aux Champs-Elysées* (1687), reprinted in a special Lully issue of *La Revue Musicale*,

January 1925, p. 90. I have translated passages from the first edition of Antoine Bauderon De Sénecé, *Lettre de Clement Marot a Monsieur de . . . touchant à ce qui s'est passé à l'arrivée de Jean Baptiste de Lulli, aux Champs Elysées* (Cologne, 1688), pp. 32–33, 51–53. For Le Cerf's theory of Cambert's death, see Le Cerf de la Viéville de Fresneuse, *Comparaison de la musique italienne et de la musique française*, 2d part (Brussels, 1705), p. 177. The Brothers Parfaict are quoted in Pougin, op. cit. supra, at p. 250, note (1). See also Romain Rolland, *Les Origines du Theatre Lyrique Moderne—Histoire de L'Opéra en Europe Avant Lully et Scarlatti* (Paris, 1931), p. 259, note (3). An example of the "heartbreak" theory of Cambert's death is found in Castil-Blaze (François Henri Joseph Blaze), *Molière Musicien* (Paris, 1852), vol. 2, p. 126.

London Records

In the course of my researches, I reviewed all of the parish records published by the Harleian Society as well as the unbound parish records for London and Middlesex County in the possession of the Society for Genealogists in London. I also consulted will records at the Guildhall Library, County Hall, and the Middlesex Record Office. The reference to Marianne Cambert's passport is in Calendar of State Papers, Domestic Series March 1, 1678 to December 31, 1678 (London, 1913), p. 614. The record reflects the grant of a passport to "Marie du Moulier and Marianne Cambert." It is possible that the first name is a misprint of the maiden name of Cambert's widow, Marie de Moustier.

I am indebted to Stephen Goslin, Records Agent for the search of the King's Bench Records.

Nationalistic Criticism in England and France

The comments of Sir John Hawkins are drawn from his *A General History of the Science and Practice of Music* (London, 1776), vol. 4, p. 239 (footnote). For Bourdelot's republication of Le Cerf's innuendo, see *Histoire de la Musique et de ses Effets, depuis son origine, jusqu'à présent*, begun by Pierre Bonnet and Abbe Bourdelot and completed by Jacques Bonnet (Amsterdam, 1725), vol. 3, pp. 163–64.

Charles Burney also cites a French music history source for the statement that "Cambert, who died in London in 1677, broke his heart on account of the bad success of his operas in England." Charles Burney, *A General History of Music from the Earliest Ages to the Present Period* (London, 1789), vol. 4, p. 188.

Fouquet's Trial in the Letters of Madame de Sévigné

All quotations from letters of Madame de Sévigné relating to the Fouquet trial (and to the execution of the Marquise de Brinvilliers) are taken from *Selected Letters of Madame de Sévigné*, translated by H. T. Barnwell (Everyman's Library: London, 1960).

Among the principal sources on Fouquet's trial are:

Clément, Pierre. *Histoire de Colbert et de son Administration*. 2 vols. Paris, 1874. Vol. 1, pp. 89–147.

Lair, J. *Nicolas Fouquet*. 2 vols. Paris, 1890.

For Colbert's campaign against Fouquet, see also Clément, Pierre, *La Police sous Louis XIV*. Paris, 1866. Sainte-Beuve's judgment on Madame de Sévigné's response to the Breton unrest is drawn from Sainte-Beuve, *Selected Essays*, translated by Francis Steegmuller and Norbert Guterman (London, 1965), p. 131.

The Janitor's Story: An Ethical Dilemma in the Harvard Murder Case

The two principal contemporary accounts of the Harvard Murder case are found in:

Bemis, George. *Report of the Case of John W. Webster*. Boston, 1850.
Stone, James W. *Report of the Trial of Prof. John W. Webster*. Boston, 1850.

I thank my good friend, the Cleveland antiquarian bookseller Peter Keisogloff, for bringing to my attention the trial scrapbook of A. Oakey Hall, which is now in my collection.

Modern works on the case include:

Dilnot, George. *The Trial of Professor John White Webster*. New York, 1928.
Sullivan, Robert. *The Disappearance of Dr. Parkman*. Boston, 1971.
Thomson, Helen. *Murder at Harvard*. Boston, 1971.

The political career of A. Oakey Hall is recounted in Croswell Bowen's *The Elegant Oakey* (New York, 1956).

For an excellent study of ethical issues concerning the defense of the Courvoisier case, see David Mellinkoff, *The Conscience of a Lawyer* (St. Paul, 1973).

The recent case of *Lowery* v. *Cardwell*, 575 F.2d 727 (9th Cir. 1978) demonstrates that Charles Phillips's dilemma is still very much with us. In this case defense counsel abruptly broke off direct examination of the defendant when she testified (falsely, in his view) that she had not shot the decedent. Then in chambers counsel moved the trial judge (who was the fact finder) that he be permitted to withdraw from the case but did not state any reason. His motion was denied. Returning to the courtroom, he quickly brought the direct examination to an end and never referred in his brief closing argument to his client's denial. The Court of Appeals commended counsel for his ethical concern about lending assistance to perjury, but held that the motion to withdraw made under these circumstances denied the defendant a fair trial. See also *Colorado* v. *Schultheis*, Colorado Court of Appeals, No. 78-298 (July 10, 1980).

The Trial of Jane's Aunt

The contemporary account of the trial on which this essay is based is *The Trial of Jane Leigh Perrot, taken in court by John Pinchard* (Taunton, 1800), of which I have a copy in my collection. Although I disagree strongly with his apparent belief in Aunt Jane's innocence, I have also drawn material on the background of the case and quotations from Austen-Leigh family papers from Sir Frank Douglas MacKinnon's *Grand Larceny: The Trial of Jane Leigh Perrot* (London, 1937). *Grand Larceny* contains a facsimile of the Pinchard trial pamphlet.

Biographical and critical works I have consulted include:

Apperson, G. L. *A Jane Austen Dictionary*. London, 1932. Pp. 11–17.

Austen-Leigh, James Edward. *Memoir of Jane Austen*. Oxford, 1926.

Austen-Leigh, William and Austen-Leigh, Richard Arthur. *Jane Austen: Her Life and Letters, A Family Record*. 2d ed. New York, 1965. Pp. 126–40.

Jenkins, Elizabeth. *Jane Austen*. New York, 1949.

Laski, Marghanita. *Jane Austen and Her World*. New York, 1969. Pp. 43–44.

Pinion, F. B. *A Jane Austen Companion*. London, 1973.

Michael Gilbert's "A Case of Shoplifting" appears in *Ellery Queen's Mystery Magazine*, May 1976, pp. 6–12.

Gilbert and Sullivan on Corporation Law:
Utopia, Limited and the Panama Canal Frauds

Biographical and critical sources quoted in the article are:

Baily, Leslie. *The Gilbert & Sullivan Book*. London, 1952. Pp. 212, 213, 400.

Darlington, W. A. *The World of Gilbert and Sullivan*. New York, 1950. Pp. 173–74.

Pearson, Hesketh. *Gilbert: His Life and Strife*. New York, 1957. Pp. 19, 83, 264–65.

Shaw on Music. Edited by Eric Bentley. New York, 1955. Pp. 216, 219.

For the history of the Companies Act, see *Palmer's Company Law*, 21st edition, edited by Clive M. Schmitthoff and James H. Thompson (London, 1968), pp. 5–9; Sir William Holdsworth, *A History of English Law*, edited by A. L. Goodhart and H. G. Hanbury (London, 1965), vol. 15, pp. 49–59.

For *Punch*'s review of *Utopia*, see *Punch*, 105, October 28, 1893, p. 204. Despite its critical rejection of *Utopia*, there is evidence that Gilbert's corporate satire became a part of the magazine's comic world view. A cartoon published three years later depicts a proposed financing of the Ottoman Empire by the Western Powers. The Ottoman Empire is shown being reorganized as a corporation under the name "Turkey, Limited." *Punch*, 111, November 28, 1896, p. 259.

For a report of the Glasgow Bank trial, see *Trial of the City of Glasgow Directors*, edited by William Wallace, Notable Scottish Trials (Glasgow-Edinburgh, 1905). See also Major Arthur Griffiths, *Mysteries of Police and Crime*, 2 vols. (London, 1899), vol. 2, p. 390.

An account of the Panama Canal scandal is provided in Maron J. Simon, *The Panama Affair* (New York, 1971). Many of the facts relating to the Panama case to which I make reference are drawn from Mr. Simon's interesting book. For an eyewitness report of the Panama trials, see Albert Bataille, *Causes Criminelles et Mondaines de 1893* (Paris, 1894), pp. 1–314.

The Unpleasantness at the Garrick Club

The principal Victorian sources relating to the Garrick Club controversy are:

Fitzgerald, Percy. *The Garrick Club*. London, 1904. Pp. 54–71.

Yates, Edmund. *His Recollections and Experiences*. 2 vols. London, 1884. Vol. 2, pp. 1–37.

For treatment of the controversy in modern biographies of Dickens and Thackeray, see:

Johnson, Edgar. *Charles Dickens: His Tragedy and Triumph*. 2 vols., New York, 1952. Vol. 2, pp. 929–36.

Ray, Gordon N. *Thackeray: The Age of Wisdom (1847–1863)*. New York, 1958. Pp. 278–90.

Quotations from Thackeray's letters are generally drawn from *The Letters of William Makepeace Thackeray*, 4 vols., edited by Gordon N. Ray (Cambridge, Mass., 1945).

Certain references to Garrick Club history are found in: Fitzgerald, op. cit.; Timbs, John, *Clubs and Club Life in London* (London, 1908), pp. 218–27.

For Harry Furniss's comments on Yates and the Garrick affair, see his *The Two Pins Club* (London, 1925), pp. 44–66. Robert Louis Stevenson's glee over Yates's libel conviction is mentioned in Furnas, J. C., *Voyage to Windward: The Life of Robert Louis Stevenson* (New York, 1951), p. 213.

"Under Sentence of Death": Some Literary Views on Capital Punishment

For the exchange of views on the validity of Professor Ehrlich's studies, see *Yale Law Journal* 85 (1975–76): 164–227, 359–69.

Dwight MacDonald's "The Triumph of the Fact: An American Tragedy" originally appeared in *The Anchor Review*, No. 2 (1955), pp. 113–44.

Eighteenth-century sources are Henry Fielding's *An Enquiry Into the Cause of the Late Increase of Robbers* (London 1751); and Boswell's *Life of Samuel Johnson*. Page references to the Modern Library edition of Boswell are as follows: Most hanged criminals have "never thought at all," p. 357; Johnson's intervention for Dr. Dodd, pp. 707–14; Johnson's lament for the abolition of the procession to Tyburn, p. 1033.

Nineteenth century sources are: Trollope, Frances, *Domestic Manners of the Americans*, edited by Donald Smalley (New York, 1949), pp. 163–166. Thackeray: *The Case of Peytel* (1839); *Going to See a Man Hanged* (1840). Dickens: Letters to the *Daily News* of 28 February, and 9, 13 and 16 March, 1846 (advocating the abolition of capital punishment); letters to the *Times* of 14 and 19 November, 1849 (letters against public hanging inspired by Dickens's attendance at the execution of the Mannings).

The remarks of the "debilitated cousin" on capital punishment appear in chapter 53 of *Bleak House*.

Twentieth century sources:

Camus, Albert. "Reflections on the Guillotine." In *The World of Law*. 2 vols. Edited by Ephraim London. New York, 1960. Vol. 2, pp. 512–52.

Koestler, Arthur. *Reflections on Hanging*. New York, 1957.

Koestler, Arthur, and Rolph, C. H. *Hanged By the Neck*. Penguin Special Edition. Baltimore, 1961.

Orwell, George. "A Hanging." In *Decline of the English Murder and Other Essays*. Penguin Books. Harmondsworth, 1965. Pp. 14–19.

Albert Borowitz has been described by a critic as a "sleuth upon the crossroads between literature and crime." In *A Gallery of Sinister Perspectives: Ten Crimes and a Scandal,* Mr. Borowitz further explores these intriguing crossroads through a series of studies of writers, intellectuals and musicians who directly confronted crime in their own lives or were inspired by actual criminal cases to create significant works of the imagination.

Among the figures in his "gallery of sinister perspectives" (a phrase used by Henry James to describe crime history), Mr. Borowitz shows us the brilliant nineteenth-century Swedish novelist, educator and penologist C.J.L. Almquist under indictment for attempted arsenic poisoning; Harvard professor John Webster clumsily disposing of the body of an importunate creditor; an historian and a social reformer of the Sung Dynasty in bitter conflict over the fate of a country girl who cut off her suitor's finger; the aunt of Jane Austen defending a capital charge of shoplifting in eighteenth-century Bath; and the shrewd and enchanting Mme. de Sévigné commenting on the course of the trial of her friend, fallen Finance Minister Fouquet, for embezzlement and treason against Louis XIV. A fantastic counterpart to these accounts of historical criminal cases is provided by an analysis of the scurrilous legend of the murder of a French opera composer by Jean-Baptiste Lully, a seventeenth-century antecedent of the Mozart-Salieri myth.

The studies of works inspired by criminal cases include essays on one of the supreme masterpieces in this genre, Browning's *The Ring and the Book,* and on the literary and operatic portrayals of Beatrice Cenci, the famous parricide of Renaissance Italy; and a survey of literary views of capital punishment over the last three centuries. From the